W9-BGI-264

Our community's compassion runs deep.
For 150 years, the Oregon Humane Society-
SPCA has embodied each generation's determination
to save lives, stop suffering, and bring loving
best friends to our families.

Pioneering Compassion

150 Years At The Oregon Humane Society

©2018 by The Oregon Humane Society

All rights reserved.

No part of this book may be reproduced in any form without written permission from the publisher.

Printed in PRC.

ISBN 978-0-692-98778-0

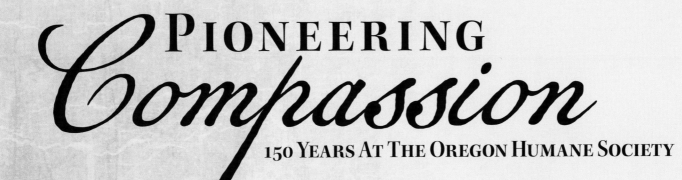

PIONEERING
Compassion
150 YEARS AT THE OREGON HUMANE SOCIETY

Written and edited Mary Henry and
Elizabeth Mehren with the OHS History Corps

Graphic Designer Scott Rubens

Photo Editor Tim Hurtley

Profiles contributed by Kathy Eaton and Ed McClaran

This book is dedicated to all the people who have made the Oregon Humane Society the remarkable institution it is today, but mostly...

In loving tribute to all the pets who have found shelter here

Table of Contents

For 150 years, the Oregon Humane Society has stood for kindness and compassion.

*The mission of the Oregon Humane Society is to
foster an environment of respect, responsibility
and compassion for all animals through education,
legislation and leadership; to take care of the homeless,
to defend the abused, and to fight with unrelenting
diligence for recognition of the integrity of all animals.*

2 Acknowledgments

THE MAGIC OF THE OREGON HUMANE SOCIETY IS CONJURED THROUGH LOVING CONNECTIONS.
THE BOOK YOU HOLD IN YOUR HANDS CELEBRATES AND EXEMPLIFIES THE OHS SPIRIT OF COLLABORATION.

My determination to share the long and storied history of OHS stemmed from a desire to counteract outdated stereotypes and to help people understand the broad range of services we offer today. I want those who have been with us for decades to take pride in our clean, bright state-of-the-art facility, where we save virtually every life. I want those new to our community and those who come after to understand that it was not always this way, and how this victory was won.

Thanks to early encouragement and generous support from Judith Wyss, I was able to take a hiatus from my usual duties at OHS to focus on researching our history, and began to compile some of the stories you see in this volume. I also recruited the History Corps, a group of OHS volunteers who contributed their unique talents to our sesquicentennial publication. It has been such a pleasure to work with each person on this formidable team:

Judy Anderson: if you ever write a book, may you have a reference librarian like Judy on your team. From administering our online collaboration to sharing her professional research skills, she has been a ready source of knowledge and expertise.

Deanna Cecotti, who uncovered hidden treasures in the humane society's records at the Oregon Historical Society.

John Cushing, who explored Thomas Lamb Eliot's papers at Reed College and focused his keen copy editor's eye to improve this manuscript.

Kathy Eaton, whose organizational drive moved us forward, and whose journalistic skill captured fascinating characters who have been an important part of our history.

Alyce Forsythe, who added context to our understanding of our founders and scanned endless newspaper clippings.

Tim Hurtley, a proud Oregon native, who preserved irreplaceable paper documents electronically for future generations and prepared photos for publication.

Ariella Jochai, whose research showed us the face and words of our founder, Thomas Lamb Eliot.

Ed McClaran, who applied his passion for location, professional knowledge of aerial photography and friendly acquaintance with the Portland City Archives to document the history our land and buildings and our board leaders.

Special thanks also are owed to:

Elizabeth Mehren, who joyfully shared her professional expertise to create from our enthusiasm a story you want to know, in a voice you want to hear.

Lydia Bello, for her painstaking research on the Ensign Fountain.

Jules Filipski and Elerina Aldamar of the Oregon Historical Society Research Library; Mary Hansen, Assistant Archivist, City of Portland Archives & Records Center; Multnomah County Records Management and Archives; and Jim Carmin, Special Collections Librarian of the Multnomah County Library Rare Book Room, who safeguard the treasures of our past and supported our work with wisdom and patience.

Gay Walker, Special Collections Librarian, Reed College, for the voluminous research material she provided on Thomas Lamb Eliot.

Executive Director Kerry Tymchuk and the staff of the Oregon Historical Society.

Bernie Unti of the Humane Society of the United States and Stephen Zawistowski, Ph. D. CAAB, Science Advisor Emeritus of the ASPCA, who shared generously of their expertise about the broader history of animal welfare, and Joyce Briggs, who introduced us.

Sean Sterling and *The Oregonian*, for sharing their historic reporting and authorizing OHS to reprint articles and photographs for this publication.

Maine's Vinalhaven Historical Society for early photos of the Ensign Fountains.

I am grateful to all those who shared memories, submitted photographs, asked questions and provided guideposts.

This book would not have been possible without the contributions of all those, mentioned and unmentioned, whose dedication, compassion and generosity have made the Oregon Humane Society what it is today, and what it will be in the future.

Mary Henry, OHS Associate Director of Major Gifts

BY SHARON HARMON, OHS PRESIDENT & CEO

I spend a good deal of time in the future, envisioning tomorrow's world for animals—a future so bright our founders could only come close to imagining it. I like to think they would approve of our progress since the day in July 1989 when I first walked into an old, smelly, falling-down shelter filled with so many beautiful pets, as well as a raft of creative, committed, caring and compassionate people dedicated to helping them. Together, we've built a state-of-the-art animal shelter and first-of-its-kind Animal Medical Learning Center that draws acclaim from around the globe. Together, we've saved hundreds of thousands of lives, thanks to dedicated volunteers, talented staff, visionary board members, and most of all, the generous people of Portland and surrounding communities who have built this institution through support and dedication to the animals and region we serve.

My twenty-nine years at OHS are only a fraction of the time this venerable institution—one of the oldest in Oregon—has been helping "every living creature," as they said back in the 1930s. Although my focus remains on building an ever-brighter tomorrow for animals and the Oregon Humane Society, it is of great value to understand how much we owe to the pioneering founders who started our organization and to the dedicated people who carried us through the difficult decades of pet overpopulation, now thankfully becoming a thing of the past. Today, we can take pride that our community is recognized as one of the best places in America for shelter pets, and our organization is highly regarded locally, across the nation and beyond for innovative programs to care for animals.

As we approach the end of pet overpopulation in our community, the Oregon Humane Society can now return to the heart of our original mission: ending animal suffering. As long as there are homeless pets who need us, OHS will care for them as our own and find families who will love them forever. Through anti-cruelty work and helping animals overcome behavioral and medical challenges, by standing up for pets who have no-one else and educating a new generation to carry on our work, we will build that bright future together. Looking at the progress we've made so far, I can only imagine what the next century and a half will bring.

Sharon M. Harmon

Today's state-of-the-art shelter is a testament to OHS's forward-thinking leadership and a generous animal-loving community.

Introduction

This is the story of a remarkable Oregon organization, an institution almost as old as the state itself. On Valentine's Day in 1859, Oregon became the thirty-third state to join the Union. Just nine years later, a 27-year-old clergyman and humanitarian named Thomas Lamb Eliot gathered a handful of like-minded citizens to establish the group that grew into the Oregon Humane Society. It is said that Eliot was moved to create an entity devoted to animal protection after witnessing a horse being brutally beaten on a city street. "Must do something for horses here!" Eliot noted to himself.

Portland was a remote outpost at the time, with unpaved roads and only 6,700 residents. And yet, concern for animals had already become a priority. In what very well may have been a precursor to what is known now as "the Oregon way," these early settlers confronted harsh demands in their new Northwest home. Their pioneering spirit led them to look beyond accepted norms, and to think independently about life, and about the animals with whom we share our lives. As it has with each successive generation, OHS reflected a fundamentally Oregonian set of values, neither sentimentalizing nor objectifying animals, but recognizing the special bond between humanity and the animal world. From the outset, the central concern at OHS has been compassion. But kind-heartedness and benevolence also translated to legislative advocacy. Leaders of the fledgling Oregon Humane Society sat down with members of the early Oregon legislature, determined to make sure that the welfare of animals and children was woven into the state's legal fabric.

Thomas Lamb Eliot was just 27 years old when he helped found the Oregon Humane Society.

Through the decades, community leaders like these have made OHS what it is today.

FUN FACT

An estimated 462,000 dogs and 505,000 cats lived in the Portland/ Vancouver metro area in 2016.

As new as Oregon was, this made OHS the fourth organization founded in the country devoted to the care of companion and draft animals, along with livestock—and, in its early days to the welfare of children as well. Founded only months after the San Francisco SPCA, OHS is the oldest animal welfare group in the Northwest. Indeed, OHS is only two years younger than the American Society for the Prevention of Cruelty to Animals, founded in New York City in 1866.

All of which raises the question: What is it about the home of OHS, Portland—and for that matter, about the state of Oregon as a whole—that fosters such fondness for animals? Why did these early citizens of Portland make animal protection a civic priority? Why do animal sculptures—beavers, deer, bears, ducks, birds, pigs and more—abound on the streets of Portland? What prompts business owners throughout the city to place water bowls for dogs outside their front doors? What gave OHS, among all other U. S. humane organizations, the temerity to establish a goal of ending pet overpop-ulation—and then, to actually achieve that aim? How did OHS become the nation's first animal shelter that provides residential training and housing for veterinary students from one of its fine public universities, Oregon State University? What other U. S. city has a café called Purringtons Lounge that offers craft beer, shelter cat adoption and "purr yoga"? Why are dogs seen splayed out on the sidewalks in Portland as their owners sip espresso or indulge in something stronger at happy hour? Who thought to place poo-poo bags in so many parks and pathways in Portland (and not incidentally, most Portland pet owners dutifully employ them).

There is, of course, no single answer to any of these questions. By nature, Oregonians are a hardy lot, like the horses and oxen that carried pioneers and their possessions to this brazen Northwest Territory. Early settlers who survived the difficult covered-wagon journey to reach the West turned right to head to the lush forests and wild, wide spaces of Oregon, not left toward the promise of riches in the California Gold Rush. Wagon wheel ruts on the trail to Oregon had paw prints beside them. Along with their hopes and dreams for life in a strange and unknown land, these pioneers brought their dogs.

Still earlier, the explorers Meriwether Lewis and William Clark treated Seaman, their Newfound-land dog mascot and companion, with the same love and respect that they extended to one another. Venturing back even further into history, deep into the Paleolithic era, Portland novelist Jean Auel imagined the first prehistoric partnership between canines and humans. When she penned "The Clan of the Cave Bear," the first of her extraordinarily successful "Earth's Children" series, Auel was living in the city's Goose Hollow section.

Se-Cho-Wa (seated), who remembered seeing Lewis & Clark, is interviewed by Mrs. Eva Emery Dye while a dog sleeps in the foreground.

Movie star Rin Tin Tin traveled to OHS to pay his respects at the grave of Bobbie of Silverton.

Bobbie the Wonder Dog became a national sensation in 1923 when he made his way home to Silverton, Ore., after becoming separated from his family on a road trip in Indiana. It took Bobbie six months to forge the 2,551-mile journey, through plains and deserts, across deep valleys and up and down tall mountains. Bobbie's trek was so celebrated that he played himself in a 1924 silent movie, *The Call of the West*. After he died in 1927, Bobbie was buried with honors on the grounds of the Oregon Humane Society. No less a celebrity than Rin Tin Tin visited the cemetery to place a wreath in Bobbie's memory.

OHS has ended the suffering of stranded whales and protected their rights on movie sets. Twice, OHS housed an elephant for the Portland Opera. When a collection of giant macaws was discovered in a condition of neglect, OHS stepped in to rescue them. OHS has hired cowboys to tend to starved cattle, and has freed horses from cruelty and the occasional flood. For years, OHS operated a "lollipop farm" so city kids could get acquainted with rescued donkeys, goats, horses and other farm animals.

The Lollipop barn.

Across Oregon animals have dutifully served as protectors, fire lookouts, rodent controllers, livestock herders, and of course, beloved companions.

If "What is it about Portland and its dogs, cats and other creatures?" were a pop quiz, here are some possible answers, solicited in an entirely unscientific fashion from random Portlanders:

"We love the outdoors here. Just look at how much open space there is in Portland alone. Exploring the outdoors with a dog is just so much better than doing it alone."
~ Carolyn, fourth-generation Portlander

"People move here—I know we did—because of the proximity to the outdoors. The area does seem made for people with pets."
~ Veronica, a veterinarian

"In Portland, we love our gardens. We like to be outside, digging in the dirt, planting new flowers and trees. Having a dog alongside for that work makes it not feel like work."
~ Bill, retired professor

In Portland our identity is not tied up with what we do, and certainly not what we do for a living. When was the last time someone asked you what you 'do'? The preferred question here is 'what do you like to do?'

"People in Portland are living life now, not judging others on the basis of what they have done, where they went to school, who their ancestors were. If you have a dog or cat or pygmy pig or whatever, well then, so much the better."
~ Rebecca, a psychologist

Majestic Timberline Lodge and a helpful Husky trail dog drew US Senator Adlai Stevenson to Oregon in the 1950s.

This big fuzzy dog shared the Governor's mansion with Gov. Robert D. Holmes and his wife Marie in the 1950s.

"Caves," said Scott, who works in aviation. "With our winters we are essentially cave dwellers. Who shares our caves? Our dogs and cats, companionate animals. And when we emerge from our caves to take our pets for walks, we engage with other pet-accompanied cave dwellers, out for the same purpose."

"Why do we like animals so much in Portland? I don't know, I don't know the answer to that question. Maybe it's because we drink so much coffee."
~ Shelley, Jack Russell terrier owner

Not all the attention on animals has been so affirmative. The first mention of dogs in an Oregon newspaper came on Feb. 5, 1846, when the *Oregon City Spectator* urged the city government to "tax dogs, prohibit hogs and"—newspapers needed to make money, even then—"advertise in the *Spectator*." A month later, the *Spectator* continued its cavalier canine coverage with a story reflecting the casual cruelty of the time:

"A man had just received a large pot of lobsters, fresh and lively, when a boy stood looking at the critters, accompanied by his dog. 'Suppose you put your dog's tail between the lobster's claws,' said the man. 'Agreed,' said the boy. The peg was extracted from the claw, and the dog's tail inserted. Away went the dog off home, howling at the squeeze his tail got from the lobster. 'Whistle your dog back, you young scamp, you,' cried the man. 'Whistle your lobster back,' cried the boy, and absquatulated. The boy made a lobster supper that night."

Still, in lumber camps, on fishing vessels, on farms, ranches and encampments and in villages, towns and today's modern cities, animals in Oregon have dutifully served as protectors, fire lookouts, rodent controllers, livestock herders and of course, beloved pets. The Oregon Humane Society's steady record of success is built on Oregonians' deep bonds of compassion and caring for the animals who have always—reliably, unconditionally and remarkably—shared our lives.

These 19th century Oregon adventurers would not have dreamed of scaling this mountain without their faithful dog.

5 Long Long Ago

The prehistoric fiction of Oregonian Jean Auel was rooted in archaeological fact. Long before Auel's fictional characters wandered the plains of what is now Europe, "bear dogs" and large prehistoric cats occupied the Northwest. As the mountains of the Cascade and Coast Ranges rose 44 million years ago, ancient relatives of modern companion animals lived in the land that became Oregon. Fossils of distant relatives of today's cats and horses abound in the John Day Fossil Beds. The details are still debated, but 30,000 years ago or more, a subspecies of Eurasian wolf began interacting with humans, perhaps foraging for food around human campsites. And when people migrated to North America around 14,000 years ago, they brought domesticated dogs with them.

"Dogs seem to have a very special place in human communities in the past," according to University of Alberta archaeologist Robert Losey. Five to eight thousand years ago, humans were reverently burying the dogs who shared their lives. "Globally, there are more dog burials in prehistory than any other animals, including cats and horses," Losey has said. When they laid their dogs to rest, early hunters and gatherers ceremoniously placed necklaces, bowls and bones into the gravesites. Chemical analyses of these ancient dog remains show that they were eating a diet quite similar to that of the humans they lived with. Even at a spiritual level, in Losey's view, these prehistoric people knew their dogs as "unique, special individuals."

On the feline front, cats have shared life with humans for eight to twelve thousand years. While dogs have evolved into many shapes, sizes and characteristics, domestic cats have remained more similar to their ancestors in form and behavior. Some scholars think people deliberately tamed cats in order to hunt vermin. Others maintain that humans came to accept the presence of cats because they helped control the rodent population. No matter who chose whom, the feline-human bond proved deep and meaningful.

These Native Americans and their dogs continue a long history of interdependence.

Their mascot dog had a place of honor atop the Sellwood firefighters' horse-drawn wagon.

6

Compassionate Pioneers

"There have been humane sentiments cropping out here and there all along the world's history, but not until the philosophy of well-organized humane societies, supported by law, came to its aid did it make noticeable progress… Out of information comes emotion, out of emotion comes action."

~ OHS Founder William T. Shanahan, 1888

Oregon Journal reporter Frances Blakely was also a longtime OHS trustee. Blakely served with some of the group's founding members, including Thomas Lamb Eliot. In 1948, she wrote this story about the "boy minister" who started OHS and how "needless cruelty to Portland animals" was brought to a halt.

OHS founder Dr. Thomas Lamb Eliot gathered twelve like-minded men to establish the state's first animal welfare organization in 1868.

William M. Ladd — George H. Himes — J. K. Gill — Sylvester Farrell — Col. Henry E. Dosch — Joseph Simon — H. W. Corbett — Henry Failing — A. L. Mills — Rev. William G. Eliot

THE MEN shown above were—with one exception—among those who helped Dr. T. L. Eliot organize the humane society. Exception is the Rev. William G. Eliot, son of the founder, who recently revealed facts told in the story below.

'Boy Minister' Launched 'Humanity' In Oregon

How was needless cruelty to Portland animals in the "good old days" stopped?

Here are the details of the courageous battle and the men who fought it to a successful conclusion, as written from recently revealed notes made 81 years ago.

By FRANCES BLAKELY

"**M**UST do something for horses here!"

This line, scribbled in the notebook of a 26-year-old Unitarian minister, as he was riding from the dock where the ship berthed that had brought him to Portland, was the beginning of the Oregon Humane society.

On a November night in 1868 this one minister and 12 Portland business men organized the Oregon Humane society.

They met in a church and opened the meeting with prayer.

Portland was a village of 5000 souls living in houses huddled on the Willamette river bank.

PRINCIPAL credit for founding Oregon Humane society is due to Dr. Thomas Lamb Eliot, the "boy minister."

ONE OF THE OCCUPANTS of the humane society's animal harbor these days is "Freckles." English setter who was so kindly toward his traditional prey (as shown above) that his owners turned him out of their home.

SUNDAY, DECEMBER 12, 1948 Oregon Journal—3

These early leaders of the humane movement in Oregon were the same ordinary citizens who introduced child protection and labor laws to the fledgling state. While Simon Benson installed now-iconic fountains to provide workers with water to prevent them from imbibing on the job, OHS placed beautiful specially designed watering stations for horses and dogs throughout the city of Portland. They sanded streets to prevent horses and their carriages from slipping in wintry conditions. They inspected meat packing and slaughter houses to protect animals from brutality and to ensure that citizens were safe from contaminated meat. They arranged care for neglected and abused children. These same citizens spent their own time and money to learn about the emerging humane movement on the East Coast. As the state government evolved, they insisted on the passage and enforcement of humane laws in their young state. Specifically, what this small but determined band of humanitarians sought was "legislation upon the matter for the passage of stringent laws which should render persons who practice heartless cruelties on the brute creation liable to severe penalties."

"Humanitarians have for a number of years past been agitating the subject of the organization of a society in the State for the prevention of cruelty to dumb animals; and have also endeavored to secure legislation upon the matter by the passage of stringent laws which should render persons, who practice heartless cruelties on the brute creation, liable to severe penalties.... Every humane citizen will rejoice that the ball has at length been set in motion, and will no doubt sympathize with and heartily cooperate in the movement."

~ *The Morning Oregonian*, announcing incorporation, Sept. 9, 1873

County incorporation was the next step. Articles of incorporation were filed with the Multnomah County clerk in September 1873 to establish what was announced in *The Oregonian* as "the first society in Oregon for the prevention of cruelty to animals.

Named in the incorporation papers were some of Portland's most prominent citizens: Bernard Goldsmith, Philip Wasserman, E. B. Babbitt, J. R. Cardwell, James Steel, J. A. Chapman, L. M. Parrish, William Wadhams, Henry Failing, J. H. Woodard, W. S. Ladd, the Rev. T. L. Eliot, William T. Shanahan, C. C. Strong and John B. Pilkington. Goldsmith became the group's first president. Failing, Cardwell, Wadhams, Eliot, Steel and Shanahan were directors.

The name they chose was the Oregon Society for the Prevention of Cruelty to Animals, whose "object, purpose and business...shall be to enforce such laws...to prevent cruelty to animals, to stimulate and encourage generally a humane and considerate treatment of the lower order of animate beings." The new organization was to be supported through public donations, and also through a portion of fines levied on those convicted of violating these new anti-cruelty laws.

1993 CHAIRMAN'S MESSAGE

125th Anniversary Annual Report

As far back as 1868, Society members stood boldly in the face of greed and misguided tradition and risked being shunned as meddlers by fellow citizens to protest the rampant abuse of animals and children in Oregon. They spent their own money and time to learn about the fledgling humane movement on the East Coast and insisted upon the passage and enforcement of humane laws in Oregon. Society members arranged care for neglected and abused animals and children taken by the police during investigations.

Early leaders of Oregon's humane movement were neither animal experts nor social workers. They were simply ordinary citizens who saw injustices and made commitments to stop them. They were ordinary citizens who introduced child protection and labor laws to the State of Oregon, and actively participated in their enforcement. They installed water fountains for horses and orphans, sanded streets to prevent horses and cars from slipping in icy conditions, inspected meat packing and slaughter houses to protect animals from brutality and citizens from contaminated meat. They took innumerable steps to assure all living creatures would have a humane and safe environment in which to live.

We are part of a tradition that has significantly impacted the quality of life in Oregon and throughout the Northwest. Government agencies now provide many of the services we once provided—child protection and support, road sanding, meat inspect, among others. They've done so for so long that we've forgotten that ordinary people, as members of the Society, introduced these services to Oregon. Our work is far from complete, and it's not yet time to celebrate, but before we continue with efforts to fill unmet needs, let's take a moment to stop to thank those most responsible for the Society's accomplishments. Step up to the mirror and say thanks to one ordinary citizen whose continued insistence on a higher quality of life for Oregonians and our animals continues to lead us to this result.

Your support means a lot.

We thank you.

~ John Deering, OHS Board President, 1993

Profile
WILLIAM T. SHANAHAN, FOUNDER

"Man is not by nature a kind animal," wrote William Thomas Shanahan, corresponding secretary of the Oregon Humane Society from the time of its inception until his death at age 74 in 1909. In an essay titled "The Law of Kindness," Shanahan made it clear that by "man," he was not speaking strictly in gender terms. "Cold at heart," he wrote as he lambasted the use of bird feathers for hats and other items of clothing, is the woman who lives for dress alone.

But with a white beard that flowed below his chin, and sharp eyes framed by thick, expressive brows, Shanahan was both kind and warm of heart. Shanahan was very much present at the conception of the Oregon Humane Society; indeed, Joseph Gaston's well-known history of Portland gives particular credit for the founding of OHS to Shanahan. His influence, however, extended beyond state boundaries. Shanahan's leadership in advocating for what were then known as "dumb animals" won him a diploma of honor from the American Humane Society, "in recognition of his long and faithful service in humane work." The document arrived only a short time before Shanahan died at the home of his son-in-law.

When Shanahan wrote to *The Oregonian* in 1912 to offer praise for ASPCA founder Henry Bergh upon Bergh's death, he could well have been speaking of himself. "Alone in the face of indifference, opposition and ridicule he began the reform which is now recognized as one of the most beneficent movements of the age," Shanahan wrote. "Through his exertion as a speaker and lecturer, but above all as a bold and fearless worker, in the streets, in the court room, before the legislature, the cause he adopted gained friends among the noblest men and women in the land."

THE LAW OF KINDNESS.

Responsibility of Man to His Dumb Servants.

A Paper Read By Mr. W. T. Shanahan Before the Oregon Humane Society in this City. A Beautiful Discourse.

Man is not by nature a kind animal. As the wild orange is bitter, and the wild olive destitute of richness, and the wild rose of perfume, so man is by nature a creature without mind and without heart. Even the children of civilized parents will stone or aim their arrow at a beautiful sing-bird, not loving any more those rare decorations of the woods than they love the serpent in the grass.

The love of all forms of destruction is in the bottom of the human heart, and long is the culture that will separate this dross from the spirit's gold. And when we have reached manhood and womanhood, and feel that the work of civilization has been accomplished in our lives, behold, a close examination of our souls shows

Longtime Corresponding Secretary William Shanahan argued for the Law of Kindness in this 1888 discourse.

With his wife, the former Harriet M. Taggart, Shanahan moved to Portland in 1866 from Cassopolis, Mich. He launched a successful business in music and art. But it was in the protection of animals that Shanahan directed what his obituary in *The Oregonian* called a "zealous interest." In his final annual report as OHS secretary, Shanahan observed "the unprecedented growth of our city"—if only he could see Portland now! All the excavation and street improvements had boosted the demand for workhorses. The building boom had "greatly overtaxed" the Society, Shanahan related, and especially the efforts of Humane Officer E. L. Crate. It was all but imperative, according to Shanahan, that an officer be detailed to the burgeoning East Side to ensure more vigilant protection of "dumb animals, man's most faithful and subservient friends." Complaints about the ill-treatment of animals were pouring in to OHS from all over the state, Shanahan went on as he called for state aid and "liberal contributions" from our citizens in order to expand the investigative services of OHS and bring offenders to justice. Shanahan also urged that humane education be included in the curricula of all Oregon schools.

But there was good news to report as well. In the past year, Shanahan noted, eight cast-iron fountains had been installed in different Portland neighborhoods, the better to provide water for thirsty work animals. Shanahan also cited OHS accomplishments for the year that included 912 cases of neglect and abuse reported and investigated, 72 horses taken off work in bad condition and 92 arrests for neglect, abuse and maltreatment.

(Continued on next page)

HUMANE SOCIETY OR SPCA?

The first animal protection groups, OHS included, called themselves societies for the prevention of cruelty to animals. As their mission broadened to encompass kindness in many forms, the term "humane society" was adopted instead. In the early 1970s we were officially "The Oregon Humane Society and SPCA, Inc.," Those who know us best just call us OHS.

(Continued from previous page)

Shanahan may have had his doubts about the benevolence of man, not to mention the perilous vanity of woman. But his own compassionate character was never in doubt. *The Oregonian* obituary lauded his efforts in passing laws "protecting dumb animals from the savage treatment of ill-tempered masters and in the vigorous prosecution of offenders" of such laws. As a mark of how much love truly dwelt in Shanahan's heart, the obituary also stated that though the official cause of Shanahan's death was pneumonia, it was generally thought that his demise had been hastened by his grief over the passing of his wife, who had died just three months earlier.

Joseph Gaston's well-known 1912 history of the city of Portland notes:

"In 1882 the society enlarged its field of service, extending its protection to orphan children, and the children of dissolute parents. The police commission recognized the work of the society and appointed special policemen to assist the officers of the society in enforcing the laws for the protection of dumb animals. Among those citizens who have been active in supporting the work of the society may be named Ira F. Powers, E. J. Jeffrey, C. H. Woodard, Daniel Sprague, T. L. Eliot and W. T. Shanahan."

OREGON HUMANE SOCIETY.

OUR THIRTY-NINE

ARTICLES OF FAITH.

WE BELIEVE IT TO BE OUR DUTY

TO STOP

1. The beating of animals.
2. Dog fights.
3. Overloading horse-cars.
4. Overloading teams.
5. The use of tight check-reins
6. Overdriving.
7. Clipping dogs' ears and tail.
8. Underfeeding.
9. Neglect of shelter for animals.
10. Bagging cows.
11. Cruelties on railroad stock trains.
12. Bleeding calves.
13. Plucking live fowls.
14. The clipping of horses.
15. Driving galled and disabled animals.
16. Tying calves and sheep's legs.

TO INTRODUCE

17. Better roads and pavements
18. Better methods for slaughtering.
19. Better methods for horse shoeing.
20. Improved cattle-cars.
21. Drinking fountains.
22. Better laws in all states.
23. Humane literature in our schools and homes.

TO INDUCE

24. Children to be humane.
25. Teachers to teach kindness towards animals.
26. Clergymen to preach it.
27. Authors to write it.
28. Editors to keep it before the people
29. Drivers and trainers of horses to try kindness.
30. Owners of animals to feed regularly.
31. People to protect insectiverous birds.
32. Boys not to molest birds' nests.
33. Men to take better care of stock.
34. Everybody not to sell their old family horse to owners of tip-carts.
35. People of all the states to form Humane Societies.
36. Men to give money to forward the good cause.
37. Women to interest themselves in this noble work.
38. People to appreciate the intelligence and virtues of animals.
39. And, generally, to make men, women and children better because more humane.

COMPLAINTS.

Complaints may be left at the Society's Headquarters, No. 72 Third street, Portland, or at Police Headquarters, for the Humane Officer.

A firm moral code outlined in the 1885 Articles of Faith captured the essence of the founders' vision.

Vigilance was on the minds of these early champions of animal welfare who met at the First Unitarian Church at SW 7th Avenue and Yamhill Street. In August 1880 the group incorporated under state law, and the modern-day descendant of their efforts is today one of the oldest extant corporations in Oregon. The group's stated goal was "prevention of cruelty of every kind, in every form, to lower animals and every living creature." At the organization's anniversary celebration in 1888, Dr. Thomas Lamb Eliot declared: "We undertake to call attention to infringements of national and state laws against cruelty to animals, and when warning is not sufficient, it is our duty to arrest and procure the conviction of the offenders. We endeavor to educate the community in humane sentiments, especially the young."

Their efforts prevailed. Records showed that by 1909, OHS was receiving half the fines levied against those convicted of animal crimes. Soon enough, there was talk of turning operation of the city pound over to the society. In a letter written in October 1913, OHS board member Robert Tucker told Portland Mayor H. R. Albee that his organization had received "all kinds of encouraging letters from good people who heartily endorse the move." Tucker expressed confidence not only that OHS could provide efficient service by managing the pound, but also provide relief for the city administration "from a very undesirable detail."

1913

In Portland, these early advocates for what were often then called, quite unapologetically, "dumb beasts" were working within a supportive community. An article in *The Oregonian*

HAPPY BIRTHDAY

On a cold night in November 1868 a group of Portland men organized the Oregon Humane Society. Portland was a city of only 5,000 citizens. The unbearable cruelty to horses led the men to organize and do something for the animals. The Society sought laws for the prevention of cruelty to animals and many of the same laws are still in effect. As the State became more populated with both people and animals, the Society expanded its role state-wide, and still remains the registered SPCA in all thirty-six counties. The Society has helped, rescued, or cared for hundreds of thousands of animals during its 112 years of animal welfare services. As the first and largest animal welfare organization it still remains a most progressive and influential SPCA. Numerous animal related organizations have organized only to disband after its leader passes on. Only the Oregon Humane Society has survived the Depression years and the War times.

The Oregon Humane Society (SPCA) has earned its rightful place as the protector of animals' rights."

~ *Your Animal's Friend* magazine, 1980

"I think it's quite remarkable that this organization is only 25 years younger than the Oregon Trail…. The Oregon Humane Society will, doubtless, be here in another 125 years, but we believe that the Society will be acting in a different capacity. No longer will we be taking in thousands more animals each year than can be placed in homes. Each companion animal will be a cherished member of a family and there will no longer be diseased and starving strays or abused pets."

~ Karen Brittain, *OHS Magazine*, 1993

from May 21, 1916, reminded readers that that day was "Humane Sunday," the capstone to the city's celebration of "Be Kind to Animals Week." The story made a point of stressing that "not alone is it dedicated to Towser or Rover or rollicking Howdy, but to cart horses and alley cats and starving cattle and the great white herons of the South who are slain for the plumage of their motherhood." The article went on to say that many Portland churches would devote that day's sermons to "the doctrine of charity, kindness and forbearance applied to the dumb beasts that can utter no plea of their own." Finally, the story included the following invocative prayer:

"To Thee, My Master, I Offer My Prayer:

Feed me and take care of me. Be kind to me. Do not jerk the reins; do not whip me when going up hill.

Never strike, beat or kick me when I fail to understand what you want of me, but give me a chance to understand you. Watch me and if I refuse to do your bidding, see if there is not something wrong with my harness or feed.

Do not give me too heavy loads; never hitch me where water will drip on me, nor where I face the wind. Keep me well shod. Don't force me along the smooth, slippery streets, and when I fall, be patient and help me, as I will do my best to keep up and serve you. Examine my teeth when I fail to eat: I may have an ulcerated tooth. That, you know, is very painful. I am unable to tell you in words when I am sick; so watch me, and I will try and tell you by signs. I suffer pain like you, but cannot speak like you.

Pet me sometimes; I enjoy it and I will learn to love you. Protect me in Summer from the hot sun. Keep a blanket on me in Winter weather, and never put a frosty bit in my mouth, but hold it in your hand a moment first.

I carry you, pull you, wait patiently for you long hours, day or night. I cannot tell you when I am thirsty; give me clean, cool water often in hot weather.

Finally, when my strength is gone, instead of turning me over to a human brute to be tortured and starved, take my life in the easiest and quickest way, and your God will reward you in this life, and in heaven. You will not consider me irreverent if I ask this in the name of Him who was born in a stable. Amen."

Even then, bureaucracy took its time to follow through on obvious good measures. It was 1917 before, "on approval of Portland voters," OHS assumed operation of the city pound. Affirmation from Portland voters was conclusive: 19,682 in favor of the proposal, and 11,358 against. As voters continued to extend the OHS contract, this meant OHS was in charge of issuing dog licenses, rounding up strays, reminding people of their legal responsibility to pay license fees, and receiving licensing fees to support the organization's work.

Collaboration between the city and the society continued smoothly, albeit with some differences on what percentage of profits from the fees should be afforded to OHS. In 1943, the partnership was extended to the entire county, since Multnomah County itself had no pound or other facility for dogs. These were the dark days when, unlike today, stray dogs were routinely euthanized. By city ordinance, owners had five days to reclaim stray dogs. But the high costs of treating severely injured animals had raised concerns. Until 1965, the policy was to send badly injured strays to the nearest veterinarian, where they were kept under sedation for five days. If unclaimed, they were then transferred back to OHS to be euthanized. At its March 1965 meeting the OHS board decided it would be more humane to euthanize these animals immediately, and the policy was changed.

OHS was growing, and so were demands from the city and county. An April 1965 board meeting brought debate over whether to build additional dog runs. "As the Oregon Humane Society, we are not obligated to operate the city dog pound," board president Lawrence Shaw declared. "If we did not have a contract with the city, we would not now be pound operators." Rather, said Shaw, donors provided funds for OHS "for humane work over the state to be used for the prevention of cruelty to animals—and people, not build a dog pound for the city." Board treasurer William Rutherford chimed in to assert that even though OHS did have the funds to pay for new dog runs, "the society must not always be the city's poundmaster. The city may build a pound of its own, as it considered doing not long ago."

Not surprisingly, friction between the city and the society ensued. City officials complained in early

June 1965, that OHS costs were getting out of hand. The city might buy its own trucks to enforce leash laws, these officials suggested, and would likely have a pound of its own within a few years. At last the contract with the city was renewed, providing OHS with $106,000 for pound operations.

Relations continued to deteriorate. The following year, 1966, OHS was informed that for the first time since 1917, when the humane society took over dog control from Portland police, trustees would no longer deal with the mayor and city commissioners, but with the police department's nuisance division. Things got so heated that a full cadre of newspaper and television reporters showed up for the June 1967 OHS board meeting. A juicy story was in store for the journalists as OHS board members declined to submit a bid to the city, arguing that the request only included dogs, and OHS served cats, horses and other animals as well. This principled stand, however, carried serious fiscal implications due to loss of funds from the contract.

But the city-society bonds were not so fast to crumble. In early 1968, City Commissioner Stanley Earl wrote to ask if OHS would consider taking on all functions pertaining to animals in Portland. These included dog bite and barking dog complaints currently handled by police, and nuisance division duties pertaining to animals. The OHS board agreed to study the proposal. With no

PORTLAND DOG POUND NOW LOCATED AT TROUTDALE

"The Portland dog pound, which has been consolidated with Multnomah County Animal Control, is now located outside of Portland in Troutdale. Many people confuse the pound with the Humane Society, but we are located at 1067 NE Columbia Blvd. in Portland and are not associated with the pound. The Society receives hundreds of calls monthly of protests of the pound being so far away in a remote area from Portland. However, these calls should be made to the officials who put the pound there, rather than to the Society, which is unable to assist the caller on this type of call."

~ *Your Animal's Friend* magazine, 1973

"On New Year's Day, the Oregon Humane Society will hang up its nets and cease collaring wayward canines for the City of Portland after 54 years as the city's dog catcher." Rumors that the shelter would close were not true. Instead, the emphasis would shift to more time for animal rescue, investigation of cruelty, caring for unwanted animals, finding animals new homes and education in care of animals…. With the ending of the city dog catcher contract, "…the society plans to increase its humane educational activities at its headquarters and in schools across the state."

~ *Your Animal's Friend* magazine, 1971

decision forthcoming, the Multnomah County Sheriff's office approached OHS about the possibility of becoming county poundmaster. The board expressed interest, and a special committee was convened to look into the matter.

The truth was—and the OHS board knew it—that the organization needed the money a city contract would guarantee. But there were details to attend to, starting with a board vote in May 1968 to terminate a contract for boarding and disposing of Clackamas County dogs. By June, OHS had secured a contract to continue providing services to the City of Portland for a fee of $115,000. Meantime, Multnomah County had made plans to build a new dog pound in Troutdale. This move set the OHS board to considering at its October 1968 meeting whether Portland and Multnomah County should combine "operation dog control."

The myth that OHS is little more than a glorified pound for dogs and cat has been hard to shake. The end of government contracts came in July 1971, when OHS decided it wanted to focus less on rounding up stray pets, and more on its core mission of helping animals directly. OHS has not had a government contract to collect strays since 1972.

OHS has not had a government contract to collect strays since 1972.

Today publicly funded animal services agencies in each county deal with lost and found pets, animal-related nuisances, and license enforcement. Still, OHS regularly receives calls from people with complaints about barking dogs or questions about whether their lost pet has been picked up. For OHS, the break with the city was a boon. In 1973, the first year after the dog-catching contract was terminated, adoptions at OHS increased by 33.4percent.

Some of this increase may have been attributable to efforts to help the public understand the difference between "stray animals" and "unwanted animals." Stray animals can be any animal who is running around at large, and must be reported to the pound. Unwanted animals are those who, for a myriad of reasons, an owner can no longer take care of. These unwanted animals could be taken directly to the Humane Society, where they stood a good chance of being adopted into a new home.

7

Compassionate Community: Leadership, Staff & Volunteers

As an independent nonprofit organization, OHS is governed by a board of trustees chosen to represent the community's interests. Members receive no compensation for their service. (A list of board presidents is included as Appendix A.) In its earliest years, OHS and its board of trustees were essentially one and the same. Trustees conducted day-to-day business and often dug into their own pockets to cover expenses. Even into the 1960s, board members sometimes concerned themselves with such mundane matters as whether to move the bookkeeper's desk upstairs to the education room, or whether to plant summer annuals in the garden. One trustee from that era proudly reported that she had sorted between 300 and 400 Humane Society poster entries. Another confidently assured the board that the present cash register was sufficient for use, after repairs.

Today the board consists of community leaders representing a broad range of experience and expertise. They serve as ambassadors and advocates for the organization, guiding governance, fund raising and long-range planning.

Overseeing the society's operations is the executive director, now known as the President and Chief Executive Officer, or CEO. As the organization has grown, so have the executive director's responsibilities. Hired away from the Missouri Humane Society in 1966, new director Warren Cox came with ideas that may seem archaic today, but at that time were welcomed as bold innovations. For instance, Cox urged the installation of new telephone lines in the office. He advocated new uniforms for employees. And imagine this, "telephones with a button system."

Longtime board member Betty Norrie (shown here with her OHS alum Sophie) is one of several past board chairs whose depth of experience guides our organization.

OREGON HUMANE SOCIETY SESQUICENTENNIAL BOARD

As OHS begins our 150th year of service, we are led by the following distinguished Board of Trustees:

John C. Gomez, *Chair*
Umpqua Bank

Samantha Hazel, *Vice Chair*
Yates, Matthews & Eaton P. C.

Stephen C. Kochis, DVM, *Secretary*
*Blue Pearl Veterinary Specialty &
Emergency Centers*

Peter Jensen, *Treasurer*
Internal Revenue Service

Harvey N. Black
Retired, Mediation Services

(Charles) Akin Blitz
Bullard Law

Steve Bloom
Portland Japanese Garden

Reginald R. Eklund
*Retired, NACCO Materials
Handling Group, Inc.*

Lindsay Ford
Sprout Tours

Marc F. Grignon, *Immediate Past Chair*
NW Equity Holdings, Inc.

Dr. John Gustavsson
Radiology Consultants, Inc.

Dave S. Hansen
Columbia State Bank

Gordon Keane
Digital Vision, Inc.

Lynn Loacker
Community Volunteer

Jacqueline C. Neilson, DVM
DACVM

Tonya Nichols
Robert W. Baird & Co.

Betty B. Norrie
*Retired, Program Director,
NCAA Foundation*

Marveita Redding
*City of Portland, Bureau of
Environmental Services*

Diane Rosenbaum
*Former Oregon State Senator &
Majority Leader*

Mary K. Slayton
Nike, Inc.

Laura Spear
Community Volunteer

Carolyn Vogt
Hyster-Yale Group, Inc.

Nancy Tonkin- Zoucha
Tonkin Family of Dealerships

DIRECTORS

We list here the names of some of the executives who have led OHS over the past century and a half. Incomplete records make it difficult to ascertain exact years of service, so they are listed in alphabetical order.

Gene R. Burgess, *Executive Director*

Warren Cox, *Executive Director and General Manager*

Harry Daniel, *President*

Dale H. Dunning, *President/Executive Director*

Sharon M. Harmon, *President & CEO*

Edward L. Hix, *Manager*

J. E. Rudersdorf, *Manager*

Edward Silva, *Manager*

Mrs. F. W. Swanton, *Manager*

Patrick E. Sweeney, *Executive Director*

Lew E. Williams, *Manager and Director*

James Zimmer, *Superintendent*

Edward Silva, Manager of the Oregon Humane Society, with five of his six children and some of their over 120 pets.

Profile

MARC GRIGNON From the Bank to the Board

When he first visited the old OHS shelter in 1980, Marc Grignon called it "the Andersonville of animal shelters." With high euthanasia rates and few adoption placements, the shelter was, in fact, a sorry place. The building dated from 1939, and whatever repairs and expansion had been done were pretty much a Band-Aid job, glued together to make it last for as long as possible, for as little money as possible. Fix-it funds were low.

"It was a pretty shoddy place," Grignon said.

Still, when "Uncle Ernie" Swigert asked the young trust officer at Portland's Bank of America to join the OHS Development Committee, Grignon agreed. It was a good fit, as Grignon was in charge of charitable trusts and endowments at his day job. Later in the decade, Grignon became friends with Sharon Harmon, then OHS operations director, when he took a spot on the building committee for the new shelter. With little working space for the committee at OHS, Grignon found mezzanine space at his bank's downtown office. He provided office equipment and even shared his receptionist with OHS. The campaign stalled until Sharon Harmon was selected as Executive Director, filling a leadership void. The new shelter opened in 2000.

Grignon joined the board in 2003, drawing on his experience as a banker to serve on the financial and development committees. Like so many others at OHS, Grignon credits the leadership of Sharon Harmon, along with the team she has built, for setting OHS apart from other shelters. He is also a fan of Barbara Baugnon, calling her "A marketing genius—a real rock star who's been effective at putting together the OHS brand."

Grignon also takes pride in the collaboration OHS has built with Oregon State University. The three-week OHS residency is so beneficial for OSU veterinary students that Grignon says the teaching hospital should be called "OHS University."

As OHS moves forward with its current "New Road Ahead" initiative, Grignon, co-chair of the Campaign Cabinet charged with funding these endeavors, points out that the goals are achievable, not excessively ambitious. "We're not building a Taj Mahal," he said as he examined expansion plans. "The buildings will be serviceable and presentable—built for what they're meant to do."

While adoption will continue as an OHS priority, Grignon sees the OHS mission broadening to include a renewed focus on investigations and animal abuse cases. With 1,000 abuse cases in 2016 alone, Grignon stresses the need for increased resources. He also hopes to see a permanent facility to house large-scale rescues.

The hoped-for OHS community veterinary hospital will help pet owners find care for their companions at an affordable price, Grignon notes.

Even early on, the initiative has full board support, Grignon said. As always, he added, OHS will not reach beyond its available resources, declaring, "Nothing gets built until the money is in the bank."

SCANDAL!

For all its remarkable achievements and pioneering efforts in the world of shelter care, OHS has not escaped the shadow of shame. A 1989 scandal involving clandestine animal roundups, unauthorized euthanizations and shoddy management practices brought OHS the kind of headlines that no organization wants.

But the uproar had a positive side. With the unceremonious ouster of the top OHS officials at the time, came a new executive director, Dale Dunning. And with him came Sharon Harmon, who served first as director of operations, then executive director and today, president and chief executive officer of the Oregon Humane Society.

A report by a consultant, Brad Quinn Post, found a surprising pattern of unauthorized euthanasia: 2,000-4,000 animals were killed each year, beginning in 1981. Post described secret roundups of cats and dogs, often at night, and clandestine euthanasia. But as disturbing as this information may have been, Post concluded that those involved were often motivated by concerns about animal overpopulation. The trapped animals received injections of sodium pentobarbital, and were then cremated.

These animals, said Dunning, "were put down by people not certified, under the cover of darkness." Dunning quickly moved to ensure that full transparency replaced any aura of secrecy. "We don't do anything here day or night that we wouldn't show you any time," he declared. That policy remains in place today.

We don't do anything here day or night that we wouldn't show you anytime.

New rules also took effect, requiring people who dropped off animals to leave their names, signatures and drivers' license numbers. In order to give owners a chance to claim their pets, swift euthanizations were eliminated. Protocol also was instituted to keep careful track of medications used in euthanizations, and to ensure that these procedures would only be performed by state-certified technicians.

Morale suffered during those dark years in the 1980s. A new staff manual and new leadership offered guidelines to a staff that had struggled with lack of direction.

"This organization suffered a body slam and we never want that again," Dunning commented.

Profile

SHARON HARMON Visionary Leader

She is firm, clear and assertive. She thinks big decisions through carefully and then engineers them with diplomacy. She runs a multimillion-dollar organization. Her schedule is crammed, filled with meetings, testimony in Salem and urgent phone calls. By common agreement, she is a force of nature.

As chief executive officer of the Oregon Humane Society, Sharon Harmon has little time for self-indulgence. But what moves her to tears is watching people adopt a pet at OHS on Christmas Eve.

"It brings me a lot of joy to see people in the lobby on Christmas Eve who are happy to adopt a pet and see animals who are equally excited to spring out of the shelter," she reflected. "Pets may not know where they're going, but they're going home for Christmas."

At her OHS gala celebration, Senator Betsy Johnson (left) congratulates Sharon Harmon on 25 years of leading OHS.

OHS was in the midst of an ugly scandal when Harmon came on board in 1989. "Thousands of Animals Killed," blared a headline in *The Oregonian* describing nighttime roundups and unauthorized euthanizations by a handful of people associated with OHS.

Harmon's previous work with the Marin Humane Society in Northern California gave her solid foundational skills in shelter management. After Harmon's father sent her the article from *The Oregonian*, Harmon wasted no time in faxing her resume to a headhunter. Harmon, who grew up in Southeast Portland, joined OHS as operations director and spent the next two years helping the beleaguered shelter recover from negative press and disheveled management.

OHS was in "a very bad place" when she arrived, Harmon remembered. Programs were antiquated, and the organizational scandal had taken a toll on staff. The physical plant, constructed in 1939, was crumbling before her eyes. Chunks of the ceiling sometimes fell into the dog kennels, and paint was peeling everywhere.

But even during those dark times, she said, donors continued to support OHS. About ten volunteers and a shelter staff of twenty stayed on. And Harmon herself saw tremendous potential among the mess she had inherited.

"I like a challenge," she explained, "and OHS did not disappoint."

At that time, animals were not vaccinated upon arrival, and many dogs and cats were automatically euthanized for minor problems such as cough or sniffles. There were far too few kennels to meet the demand. The community was reeling from the crush of pet overpopulation.

"We'd see roughly 150 cats a day at the shelter's receiving counter and walk them back to be euthanized," she said. "An outdated philosophy of shelter management started with 'No.' We had to set about changing all those things to get where we are today."

Nevertheless, she noted, OHS continued to attract visitors. "After Portlanders went to the zoo and OMSI, they'd come visit the Oregon Humane Society—a place that's been a large part of the fabric of this community."

It was little wonder that OHS could pull through a crisis that might have shuttered lesser organizations. Portland, to be clear, is cuckoo about animals in general—and pets in particular. The city ranks high among the most pet-friendly cities compared to similarly sized communities. Measurements include the number of board-certified veterinarians, animal daycare facilities, cat cafés, pet-friendly businesses or simply a general acceptance for cats, dogs and other animals as part of daily life.

"We're totally gaga about pets," Harmon said.

Portland also gets high marks as a philanthropic community. Social capital is important to people in Portland, and OHS has long benefited from this generous spirit. Harmon sees this as a two-way street, with OHS returning to the public a cause for well-earned pride.

"The Oregon Humane Society provides a great return on the public's investment and gives Portland a reason to be proud." Harmon said.

Harmon readily acknowledges that transparency is critical—the public expects to see what's under the hood. Information about what goes on at OHS is always available to the public. For instance, OHS has achieved one of the highest save rates in the nation. With vigorous support from OHS, Oregon has among the beefiest animal

protection laws in the nation. In her office, Harmon displays many of the legislative bills, framed with the pens that authorized them. Since 2005, OHS animal adoption rates have ranged from 95-98 percent. But progress, Harmon maintains, is no cause for complacency.

"We don't rest on our laurels," she said.

Harmon knows that in the future, it will be difficult to maintain such high adoption rates. Once, there was an abundance of puppies and kittens available for adoption. But an increased emphasis on the importance of spay-and-neuter practices has cut that number, as has the relative dearth of unwanted animals in Portland. Older animals or those who come to OHS from cruelty or neglect cases can

Harmon confers with builders about the new shelter project.

be harder to place than cute, fuzzy kittens or puppies. Adoption rates are bound to drop, Harmon concedes.

"With the need for rehoming declining," says Harmon, "we can focus on legacy issues that are unresolved since our founding." Harmon is nothing if not pragmatic. "To make big progress, an organization needs to have big goals," she reasons, adding, "We have the power to change everything—there are no barriers to good ideas at OHS."

A healthy, collaborative working environment at OHS encourages such confidence. In the past, OHS staffers seldom rose up through the ranks because the top executives sought real-world business skills. A different business model prevails today, with OHS providing opportunities for training and hiring staff with diverse skill sets. Harmon, congenitally modest, takes no credit for this change.

"I listened to smart people who walked this path," she demurs.

Although quick to learn from the past, Harmon is more interested in gazing toward the future. She has put humane investigations at the top of her list, arguing that delving into the reasons for and consequences of animal abuse and neglect represents the front-line connection to the OHS mission. "Save that dog from being harmed any further," she says. "Pick up the cat whose life becomes sacred again."

The flip side of investigations, for Harmon, is legislation. Working with the Oregon Legislature since 1991, Harmon has helped pass dozens of new laws to protect animals. Her legislative success on behalf of OHS is based on building trust and nurturing relationships with legislators. Cool-headed and determined, Harmon comes to legislative advocacy with mountains of preparation. She is never strident, and always keeps her focus. Her poise and insight reflect well on the organization she represents.

"We're not radical," she says. "[Legislators] can see our agenda on paper and know they can trust us. They walk a fine line to not advance animal protection ahead of enacting child protection laws."

Some in her position might be daunted by OHS' newest goal of raising $30 million for the "New Road Ahead" initiative. Harmon is unfazed. "There are plenty of people willing to make magic happen in this community," she says.

Some doubters have raised concerns about the dwindling supply of local animals available for adoption. Harmon reminds these skeptics that the shelter takes in thousands of animals from shelters across the West and elsewhere. More important, she points out, OHS was not founded as an adoption agency. Adoptions are a means to an end—a way to ensure that all animals in our community receive love and care. "With the New Road Ahead," she says, "we'll now redirect OHS resources with laser focus on the core mission and values we were founded on."

Harmon remains confident that OHS will continue to set the pace for animal welfare organizations around the country. She also feels sure of her role in leading progress at OHS.

"We can do all this," she said. "I'll be here to ensure that the New Road Ahead gets on its feet and then fix what didn't work." With the best team in place, and strengthening her relationships with animal advocates across the community, Harmon is optimistic about the future of animal welfare in Oregon and beyond.

CHIEF EXECUTIVE OFFICER'S CREDENTIALS

Sharon Harmon earned her Bachelor of Science degree in zoology (pre-vet med) from Oregon State University. She holds a certificate in nonprofit management from Johns Hopkins University and is a Certified Animal Welfare Administrator. She served on the Banfield Pet Hospital's Shelter Advisory Committee and the Society of Animal Welfare Administrators CAWA Certification Council. She is a past chair of the National Federation of Humane Societies' board of directors, and currently serves on the board of the Society of Animal Welfare Administrators. Harmon won the American Veterinary Medicine Association's Humane Award for 2008, and is nationally recognized for innovation in shelter management and program design. Harmon has served as OHS Chief Executive Officer since 1998.

ANNIE'S STORY

It's hard to miss the large oil painting of a beautiful dog that hangs on the second-floor wall outside the OHS development offices. The brass plate attached to the frame reads "Annie, OHS Ambassador 1994-2008." She was a gentle and affectionate German shepherd who served as the OHS canine ambassador for fourteen years.

OHS Executive Director Sharon Harmon and her husband, OHS Development Director Gary Kish, adopted Annie, a four-month-old shelter puppy, in 1994. At home and at the shelter, she led a terrific life. Annie took part in all aspects of OHS life—sitting in on employee interviews and staff meetings, greeting countless visitors, and appearing in advertising and promotional efforts. Annie also appeared in both Sharon's and Gary's byline pictures for their OHS magazine letters and articles. She was quite the OHS celebrity and loved by all who knew her.

Annie made national news in 1995 when she "borrowed" Sharon's parked Toyota pickup and had a fender-bender with a Volkswagen in downtown Portland. "I had just gone inside to run a quick errand and left Annie in the truck," said Harmon. "Somehow she took off the emergency brake, took it out of gear, and then managed to steer my truck across the street into a car that was about to pull out of its parking spot. She was quite a puppy." The resulting collision proved minor—neither Annie nor the driver of the Volkswagen was hurt, but the vehicles were damaged. Police gave Sharon a warning for an "improperly secured vehicle," but did not charge Annie. The dog, after all, was licensed and leashed and apparently there is no police category for "reckless driving by a dog."

By Ed McClaran

When Sharon Harmon's German Shepherd Annie passed away, the OHS Board commissioned fellow Trustee LeslieAnn Butler to memorialize this special dog with a portrait that hangs today in the OHS offices.

Throughout her years of service, Harmon and her dogs have been constant fixtures in the halls of OHS. Her days are long and demanding, filled quite often with difficult decisions involving tough questions of life and death. Harmon calls the shots when it comes time to make decisions on the budget. When OHS is in the news, Harmon often faces the media to present the facts behind dreadful cases of animal abuse, or—in happier moments—to describe the kind of miracles that make her job worthwhile.

"People often say to me, 'I couldn't do your job.' " Harmon reflected. "This always mystifies me. I find great satisfaction in what I do and am grateful that fortune and events led me to the Oregon Humane Society."

More than half the budget that Harmon manages goes to staff salaries. From junior aides at summer camp to the most senior vice presidents, OHS employs close to 200 people. This focus on human-delivered services dates back to the organization's early years. Salaries in 1919 represented 46 percent of the group's budget, not far from the present figure. But consider the difference in dollars. In 1919, the $5,438.26 allocated for salaries bought the services of an office clerk, a pick-up man, a deputy, a pound master, a veterinarian and extra help at $3.25 a day. The group's total expenditures of $11,890.78 back then would translate to $165,110 in today's dollars— as compared to the $14 million budget for 2016.

Harmon is also not alone as director in the range of her job description. Asked in 1943 to explain his duties as OHS director, Harry Daniel said the first thing he did when he arrived at 8 a.m. or earlier was check on the animals and the buildings, then review reports from pound employees. Throughout the day and into the night, he answered letters and phone calls. And he talked about his efforts

OHS staff gather to celebrate another successful year.

to reunite a sick child in Los Angeles with her dog here in Portland. Then, presumably with the hearts of his listeners softened by the sick-child-and-her-dog story, he presented the tentative budget for the next fiscal year.

And then there is the matter of public relations, also an issue that sometimes falls to the director. In 1968, board member Peter Jenkins reminded the staff of how important it was for OHS to present a cheerful public face. He said those associated with OHS "should at all times sell the place to the public by showing a friendly interest and making it appear to be a happy place." Jenkins said that if employees show an interest in their work, OHS would build up public interest on its own and would not need to turn to the press for stories.

Portland-area philanthropies often function around an unspoken spirit of reciprocity. At a 1985 auction benefiting the Oregon Museum of Science and Industry, OHS Executive Director Patrick Sweeney bought an employee workshop session for his staff. In a session that focused on job stress, dealing with the public, communications, public relations and staff teamwork, the subject of euthanasia also came up. Employees talked about the stress they felt around this issue.

Cuddling dogs (and cats) is an everyday pleasure for OHS volunteers.

A hungry dog is glad to see this smiling volunteer serving doggie dinners.

As hard working and dedicated as the staff of OHS might be, the organization might be in danger of coming to a grinding halt without its army of caring, committed volunteers. (A list of volunteers recognized in later years for award-winning service is found in Appendix B.)

There is almost no aspect of the work at OHS that is not aided by volunteers. This corps of unpaid personnel helps with receiving animals, placing animals in new homes, and care and feeding of animals. In addition, volunteers serve on the board, staff events and execute a myriad of other functions. The number of hours that these selfless volunteers provide literally doubles the work force productivity. They provide clerical support and work to promote membership enrollment.

They are humane education teachers, children's tour helpers, ambulance assistants and exhibit assistants. In 1986, General Manager Alan Thomas identified the following as top priority volunteer projects:

- **Operation of Pet Boutique**

- **Dog walkers**

- **School tours**

- **Helping the pet therapy department with nursing home tours**

- **Answering phones (Thursdays and Fridays)**

- **Helping with the lost pet helpline**

- **Reviewing lost and found reports to help match animals**

- **Transporting pets to spay/neuter clinics**

- **Building a resource library**

- **Helping with bulk mailing, such as OHS newsletters**

Records from 1990 show that OHS volunteers contributed more than 6,000 hours of service. Seventy volunteers attended that year's annual recognition event. By the end of the year, there were 145 volunteers performing duties ranging from shelter work to special events and pet-facilitated therapy.

Each year at OHS, the ranks of volunteers have swelled, and their responsibilities expanded. Consider that in 2016, 2,152 adult volunteers gave an astounding 245,013 hours of service to OHS. Their labor represents the equivalent of 118 fulltime employees who, if paid, would have cost OHS about $5.8 million. At the most recent volunteer appreciation celebration, more than 600 people gathered to honor this spirit of altruism.

Adults who are accepted as volunteers after filling out an online application attend a one-day orientation. They commit to 12 hours of service each month for a period of six months. Experienced volunteers mentor the newcomers, and advanced training classes help volunteers gain additional skills. No matter what the weather—and in Portland, that can often mean rain—these volunteers are outside morning and night, making sure the shelter dogs get exercise, attention and a chance to sniff around. In the cattery and small animal room, volunteers who provide direct care and personal attention often turn out to be among the most perceptive matchmakers, helping clients find the pets that best suit their households.

OHS community relations manager Stephanie Kittrell leads a shout-out at the annual banquet for volunteers.

Profile

VETERAN VOLUNTEER BARBRA BADER

Barbra Bader started volunteering as a dog-walker at OHS in 1989, just six months after Sharon Harmon signed on as OHS operations director. Within two years, Barbra had moved on to help with new volunteer orientation. Next, she took on pet therapy, special events, and the annual OHS telethon. Barbra had adopted her first dog in 1988 and trained the border collie/Dalmatian mix in pet therapy. For years, she and her dog worked at a drug rehabilitation site that has since shuttered.

At a time when there was no official HR director, Barbra drew on her previous experience at Tektronix, a Portland IT firm, and did human relations duties pro-bono for OHS. She served on the selection panel to hire key OHS staff members, including Barbara Baugnon, David Lytle and Kristen Bigler. Employee relations was Barbra's specialty, so she also handled the messy task of firings. She also marshaled her background to make sure government rules were followed.

Barbra has visited many shelters, comparing the standard today to what the old OHS shelter was like. When she began volunteering at OHS, the adoption office consisted of two desks, a small retail section, and "it was bedlam." Bader said the entry was noisy, cluttered and crowded. In the back, dogs were housed in a long row of kennels with little access to fresh air.

For Barbra, the most memorable achievement at OHS is the new shelter, constructed with no debt. "I can't commend/ praise Sharon Harmon enough for having a vision and implementing it," she said. Harmon looked to other organizations and adopted their best practices, Bader continued: "For example, Sharon loosened up on adoptions policies. The goal was to get animals into good homes, not strong-arm adopters. Over time, the adoption return rate dropped."

Barbra also has high praise for the investigations team and credits Harmon with growing the program to include a fully sanctioned police corps where officers work with sheriffs and police officers to get prosecutions. "The judicial system has vastly improved for animal abuse," she remarked. "We get the bad guys prosecuted and convicted."

For four years straight, Barbra has pitched in on Saturdays at the front desk. She has no plans to stop volunteering.

Youth volunteers, ages 12-17, receive hands-on training in working with animals, as well as completing projects to advance work across the shelter. Community groups are also welcomed for team-building days of service. For the entire brigade of unpaid workers, an active Facebook page builds volunteer camaraderie, and a weekly electronic newsletter called, yes, *Noseweek* keeps them posted on the latest news and volunteer opportunities.

At OHS, volunteers are rightly viewed as a kind of treasure. After an especially ardent volunteer passed away in 1995, the Bill Brock Memorial Award for Volunteer of the Year was established to honor his "passion for helping the society and the animals in its care," and his way of inspiring staff and volunteers to go above and beyond the call of duty. In 2015, OHS began awarding the Tony Platt Foster Care Volunteer of the Year, named for a young volunteer who passed away, too soon, after spending 15 months fostering a dog named Midnight who had been a victim in a criminal case.

Like any bustling, 21st-century operation, OHS would be helpless without tech assistance. Still, the transition to technology at OHS was not always smooth.

Office manager Sue Maki had her hands full, as she reported to the board in 1986:

"As most of you are aware, we have had many problems with the computer, i.e., losing information, scrambling data, etc. These problems appear to have been resolved with the purchase of a new hard drive disk."

Maki also warned: "With all the new programs being added to the computer and more people utilizing it, we will need to purchase additional printers and terminals. At this time, we are probably looking at one new printer and two or three new terminals."

Today, an IT staff of four supports more than 200 end-users, 220 computers and tablets, and 20 servers.

Together, leadership, staff and volunteers come together at the Oregon Humane Society from all walks of life, unified in their commitment to saving lives, stopping cruelty and sustaining the human-animal bond.

Volunteer Tony Platt with Midnight.

Profile
WILLIAM BOLAND
A gift of time: Profile of a public-spirited man

By Karen Inderlee
Reprinted from *OHS Magazine,*
Summer 1995

William Boland, a respected Portland attorney, has witnessed Society events first-hand for 30 years. Boland has served as a member of the Oregon Humane Society Board of Trustees, was its president and now handles wills and bequests for OHS. He has also dedicated large amounts of his time and talents to many other local organizations.

Boland attributes his drive to serve the community, in part, to growing up during the Depression, but he was also heavily influenced by an elderly attorney he met when he first started practicing law. It was during one of their first conversations that Bardi Skulison told him, "I hear that you are being asked to run for representative from your district. You better make up your mind whether you're going to be a politician or serve people." The young attorney was attracted to Skulison and his philosophy. "I made up my mind I was going to serve people and that's still my philosophy. It includes the Oregon Humane Society which was founded on the basis that it cares for all living creatures," Boland said.

An unexpected call from an old friend initiated Boland's involvement with the Oregon Humane Society. "While I was going to school I worked at the Multnomah County Library. One of the librarians was Nellie Fisher." After he graduated and started practicing law, she called him and said she'd heard that he'd been on the Zoo Commission when it first started and that he was interested in animals.

(Continued on next page)

(Continued from previous page)

"She wanted to make a will and I found out that she, too, was interested in animals, especially cats," Boland said. Fisher's will included $15,000 in stocks to OHS and the Board of Trustees was so impressed with the concern for animals that Boland had demonstrated when he handled the estate that it immediately elected him to the board. He's served the Society faithfully in many roles since that day 30 years ago.

"The interesting thing now is that I want to be a supporter of the new shelter campaign. You see, I treasure something here," Boland said, as he held up an OHS thank-you card with a picture of a dog on one side and a cat on the other. "The cat's looking at me and giving me encouragement because I'm the cat person of the Oregon Humane Society." Boland arranged for the building of the Moreland Cattery through his friend Henry Moreland.

Boland remains an influential figure of the Society's Board of Trustees. His soft-spoken manner and good humor, coupled with strong determination, have made him a wise and helpful member over the years and we're delighted to have him on our side serving the animals.

OHS staff and Board of Trustees members gratefully accept a Most Admired Non-Profit Award from the *Portland Business Journal*.

Think back to its earliest years, when OHS didn't even have an animal shelter. Back then, the founders focused on three areas: anti-cruelty legislation, law enforcement and animal welfare.

True to OHS's early core mission of protecting children and animals, J.E. Rudersdorf intervened on behalf of two children in January 1914.

Gradually, OHS began to take on responsibilities now performed by government agencies, such as dog licensing and operating the pound for local government. Today, many people think of OHS as a great place to adopt a pet. Others know that OHS investigators are in the field seven days a week to enforce the same tough anti-cruelty laws that the society has helped to enact.

But the span of work at OHS grows broader and more impressive every year. OHS is a national leader in humane education, veterinary services and hands-on education for veterinary students. OHS also has taken a lead in offering low-cost spay and neuter surgeries, behavior classes and memorial services. Through it all, OHS remains vigilant in its commitment to legislative advocacy. And that list, in truth, only scratches the surface.

Most important, in every era, the Oregon Humane Society has dedicated itself to saving lives, ending suffering and sustaining the bond between people and animals.

Toward the end of the 19th century, OHS worked closely with a single police officer designated to serve as Portland's "humane agent." This officer's duty was to patrol the city, visit city markets and produce stores and nose around wharves and excavation sites. He examined all horses and stock in the city and followed up on any complaints. He issued warnings, made arrests and aided in prosecution of offenses. Every month, he presented a full report to OHS trustees. In turn, the society itself was busy disseminating humane literature and working to educate the citizenry about animal welfare. There was much correspondence to attend to, and meetings always included hearty discussions of principles of action. Every year, the trustees offered prizes for student compositions on kindness to animals and related topics. The trustees also provided about 200 subscriptions to a publication for children called *Our Dumb Animals*. OHS officials also penned newspaper editorials inveighing against such practices as improper cattle dehorning or inadequate stabling. The trustees made sure to call attention to the "inhumanity implied" in such practices as dog or cock fighting, trap-pigeon shooting and—imagine this—the wearing of birds in women's hats. These early OHS leaders were a busy lot, also occupied with advocating for merciful slaughter methods and thoughtful disposal of abandoned or injured animals.

As the society's partnership with the City of Portland expanded, so did the scope of its endeavors. The organization provided veterinary care for the city's fire horses, street cleaning horses, a Park Bureau horse and 77 other animals. In one month in 1917 alone, OHS went on 12 ambulance calls, and investigated cases of abuse or neglect that included 245 horses, 48 dogs, 52 cattle as well as a list of 17 other animals that included goats, chickens, sheep, birds and cats. OHS officials also investigated three child welfare cases that month. That year, OHS rescued ten cows from the Columbia Slough and erected a fountain for horses and dogs on Canyon Road. A total of 968 dogs were impounded in 1917. Of those, 117 were redeemed, 274 sold and 15 escaped. The remainder died or were killed. The State of Oregon paid for OHS representatives to visit Gresham, Welches, Vancouver, St. Helens, Timber, Forest Grove, Sherwood, Troutdale, Clatskanie, Deer Island, Rose Park Station, Holbrook, Hillsboro, Pendleton, Hood River, The Dalles, Mosier, Oswego, Mt. Angel and Canby. All that in one short year, 1917.

No one could accuse the Oregon Humane Society of lacking zeal for its mission. In 1922, OHS officials joined with humane society leaders across the country to launch "crusades" against the use of monkeys by organ grinders. Humane officials also took aim at "brutal treatment of animals by showmen." As automobiles proliferated, they targeted drivers who ran over dogs or cats, "leaving their victims without offering kindly aid." It was not uncommon back in the early 1920s for OHS workers to be called on to remove pins, needles or pieces of bone that became lodged in the throats of family pets.

Portland, Ore., 1/ 31/ 14.

President and Board of Directors:

Oregon Humane Society.

The following is a report for the month of January, 1914.

No. of Calls answered during month	150
" " Horses examined	75
" " Horses laid off for minor causes	5
" " Horses destroyed	2
" " Mules examined	2
" " Dogs examined	12
" " Dogs destroyed	5
" " Dogs found homes for and otherwise relieved	7
" " Cats examined	55
" " Cats destroyed	34
" " Cats found homes for and otherwise relieved	21
" " Barns examined	3
" " Arrests	1
" " Notices posted (literature)	12
" " Miscellanous	40
" " Children cases	2
" " Ambulance	3
" " Cases unwarranted, unable to find complaint	5

Yours very respectfully,

J.E. Rudersdorf

Early in the 20th Century, OHS combatted cruelty against animals and children.

When a fishhook that a fox terrier had been playing with in 1922 became lodged in the dog's throat, who went out to administer a local anesthetic and remove "the offending object?" Why, OHS, of course. "The work is unending, night and day," an OHS notation from that year concludes.

Over the years, OHS representatives spread out across the state to help set up other humane societies. In 1970, OHS made 142 return inspections in different counties. That year, 1970, also brought 1,285 investigations, 1,442 animals treated for injury and illness and 2,071 pets returned to owner. OHS workers answered—hold on—95,502 phone calls concerning animals in 1970. They placed 12,909 pets in homes. OHS inspectors visited stables, rodeos, abattoirs, pet shops and kennels. It was a big year for shelter visitors, too—100,297, to be exact.

On and on the list went. At the end of that decade, in 1979, the organization trumpeted its accomplishments along with the programs it had initiated:

• **Full-time investigation department**

• **Animal rescue**

• **Largest animal shelter in Oregon**

• **Spay and neuter program**

• **Lollypop Farm (for unwanted and neglected barnyard animals)**

• **Burial services for deceased pets**

• **Lost and Found reports**

• **Pet Saver program**

• **Adoption program**

• **Outreach to more than 2,000 youths per month in schools and at the OHS headquarters**

• **Public information spots in newspapers, on television and on radio**

• **Legislative efforts seeking animal protection laws**

• **Weekly TV and newspaper pet programs**

• **Booths and exhibits promoting responsible pet ownership**

• **Summer library programs**

• **Senior citizen and rest home outreach**

• **Tours for children and organizations**

• **Volunteer programs**

In the mid-1980s, more than 100 years after the organization's founding, officials recognized that too many people in Portland still thought of OHS as "the dog pound," and almost everyone assumed the society was awash in tax money. Board President Tim Jones in 1985 stressed to his colleagues that not only did this perception need to be changed, but that OHS simply was not receiving the credit it deserved for all the work it did at no cost to the public.

A year later, in 1986, a growing "animal rights" movement was gaining force across America. At its May board meeting that year, OHS called on members of the public, urging them to redouble their efforts to prevent animal cruelty, more strongly oppose rodeos, increase participation in activist events and more closely collaborate and coordinate with animal welfare groups statewide. OHS officials also encouraged the public to apply increased pressure on legislators, especially concerning the matters of animal fighting and dogs riding around unsecured in the back of pickup trucks. There was also a plea for the public to encourage the Portland Housing Authority to establish reasonable guidelines for allowing pets in subsidized housing and to add a full-time cruelty investigator.

Starting with the sharp eye it has always cast on its own operations, OHS also has made a point of making sure that animal shelters—including its own—were subject to regular inspections. The Veterinary Division of Oregon's State Department of Agriculture lauded OHS in 1970:

"We use the Oregon Humane Society's facilities as an example standard for our inspections of animal shelters, pounds, kennels, pet shops, grooming parlors, zoo, etc."

~ Veterinary Division of Oregon's State Department of Agriculture, 1970

Later in the decade, Dr. Don McCoy was appointed by the OHS executive director as Animal Health Advisor. His task was to make annual inspections at OHS so that improvements could be made wherever possible.

And in its continuing advocacy for legislation designed to promote animal well-being, OHS in 2013 was successful in helping to pass an Oregon law requiring animal shelters and rescue locations to be open to inspection by local authorities. That measure came in response to a case in Brooks in which law enforcement personnel struggled to gain probable cause to search a warehouse holding more than 100 dogs.

Outreach to the public also has meant that OHS has been a national leader in raising awareness about how important it is to spay and neuter house pets. Through the "Spay and Save" program that began in 2009, OHS offers low and no-cost spay and neuter surgeries for thousands of cats and some dogs belonging to low-income families each year. OHS is one of several shelters that participate in this program through the Animal Shelter Alliance of Portland.

With its emphasis on finding homes for hard-to-place animals—rather than routinely "putting down" these cats and dogs, as is still the practice in some regions—OHS also has worked to raise awareness about ensuring a high quality of life for all creatures.

As operations director in 1994, Sharon Harmon wrote an article for the organization's magazine titled "Who Speaks For the Animals?" In it, Harmon commented on the many roles played by the organization. Sheltering unwanted and neglected animals consumed most of the group's efforts, Harmon observed. But the litany of work was long and varied, encompassing so many activities that OHS had increasingly assumed as the 20th century came to a close. All of this work, she pointed out, centered on the primary goal of actively advocating for humane treatment of animals.

Compassion's Home: OHS Land and Buildings

9

By Ed McClaran

It's fine to dream up an institution as full-service and far-reaching as the Oregon Humane Society. But then, where are you going to put it? How will you accommodate the range of humans and animals that make up an organization like this? How will you adapt to changing times, new technology, an expanding pet population and a burgeoning corps of staff and volunteers?

OHS founders scarcely needed to trouble themselves with some of these issues, since, after all, they did not even have telephone lines—not to mention slithering snakes of cables for fiber optics, wireless Internet access and who knows what else—when OHS came into existence. Broadband? Backup generators? Security systems? Pshaw, let's get on with things.

Indeed, those early OHS organizers had few spatial needs. They met regularly at the First Unitarian Church, and sometimes at the YMCA

Hall. In 1904, OHS turned up in the city directory for the first time, with an address at 350 SW Alder Street. For some of those early years, the officials migrated among several downtown spaces. By 1916, the city directory was listing OHS on SW 16th Avenue, about where the athletic fields of Lincoln High School are located today. But the prospect of taking over the operation of the City Pound meant they would need larger quarters.

1975

Residents of the area around East 50th Avenue and Powell Valley Road (now Powell Boulevard) were not happy when OHS president Albert Cowperthwait announced in April of 1916 that the society had bought a three-acre tract of land there. The parcel was intended to house an administration building, a combined hospital and stable, a series of dog kennels and runways and an operating room. Protests from the prospective neighbors were so loud and bitter that the City Council rejected the OHS proposition.

1940

FLAGS AND FLAGPOLES

In 1940, "Mr. Daniel reported that he had let the contract for purchase and placing of an 18-foot flagpole set in concrete and with iron uprights for lowering the pole. Henderson suggested that employees of the Animal Harbor be given written instructions on proper treatment of the U. S. flag and that it be raised and lowered daily with proper reverence."

In 1981, Dolores Minks donated funds to restore the flagpole on the front lawn at OHS. During the renovation process, it was discovered that the flagpole had stood since the opening ceremonies for the shelter building on June 23, 1940. On October 21, 1981, it was re-dedicated to the military K-9 Corps; a decade later, in ceremony officiated by the American Legion, a new flag was raised.

14 additional kennels. A second building housed storage and a crematory. A small shop for repairs filled a third, smaller building, while a fourth building held a two-story barn. The animal mausoleum added in 1966 was described as the first such structure in the world.

It did not take long for the society, once again, to begin outgrowing its space. In early 1970, OHS purchased an adjoining tract of about 1.5 acres for $70,000. Not long after that, an opportunity came up to buy an additional two acres.

The space was critical, as the society's work was expanding, too. A report from 1973 showed that 80,000 animals passed through the doors of OHS that year alone.

Next came the opening of the state's first humane education center, in 1978. And in 1984, OHS dedicated the Henry and Myra Moreland Cattery, tripling the shelter capacity for cats and allowing better viewing by prospective owners. Within a year of the cattery's opening, cat adoption had shot up by 38 percent.

Once again, it was time to add more space. Parking was a nightmare, and in just five years, daily phone calls to OHS had doubled. Long lines routinely formed for adoption services. A 1994 *OHS Magazine* article called "Growing Pains" addressed these concerns.

A capital campaign was announced the next year to raise funds for a 46,000-square-foot structure to replace the existing 17,000-square-foot building. The new facility would be designed to handle many more animals than the old building, which could only accommodate 4,000 pets annually. The capital campaign, led by Ernest Swigert and Dolorosa Margulis, drew more than 6,000 donors, making it one of the most widely supported projects in Oregon history for its time.

The new building produced immediate, dramatic results. Dogs in shelters are prone to a nagging condition known colloquially as kennel cough. In the new building, upper respiratory diseases in dogs dropped to an almost nonexistent level. Staff reported that the dogs, rabbits and other small pets seemed noticeably happier as well as healthier. Sales at the OHS boutique, Best Friends' Corner, skyrocketed. The number of volunteers also soared. The new cat adoption center featured double-sided kennels, as well as areas where potential adopters could visit with the kitties. And the animals had the chance to pass through what amounted to a beauty parlor, a grooming area where they could spruce up to look their best for their prospective new families.

But why stop there? In partnering in 2007 with Oregon State University's College of Veterinary Medicine to open the Animal Medical Learning

Center, OHS marked yet another national first. The teaching hospital facility allowed OSU veterinary students to work and live on site, an entirely novel concept. With its bold innovations, OHS had set a new, global standard. Australians planning to design a new shelter for Sydney, Australia, toured OHS in 2016, calling it "a benchmark for the world's best practice in animal welfare and shelter design."

It wasn't just Australians who lavished praise on the new OHS facility:

"What a World Class Shelter Looks Like"

"For about 20 years now, I have used my own 100-point shelter scoring system... My scoring scale is designed to evaluate all types of shelter on an equal footing, regardless of size, function, or budget. Very few shelters score 100 percent, but the Oregon Humane Society has now scored 100 percent three times in as many scoring visits over a 10-year span."

~ Merritt Clifton, *Animals 24-7*

In 2017, OHS has fully utilized the land acquired over the past century for buildings, dog walking path and memorial grounds. The medical center, designed to accommodate 4,500 to 6,000 patients annually, is serving twice that many. When contiguous land became available behind and to the east of the current facility, the board used reserve funds to acquire two parcels totaling approximately eight acres, a once-in-a-generation opportunity to expand our footprint and provide for the changing needs of animals.

For comprehensive information about the history of OHS land and buildings, see *oregonhumane.org/150th/book/*

"GROWING PAINS"
OHS *Animal Focus*, 1994

Can't find a place to park? Can't get through on the phone? Is the Adoption Office line out the door? It's not your imagination; we are busier than ever before.

A recent survey of our phone system found that we receive an average of 2,600 phone calls per week with a daily high of 615 calls. Contrast this with 1989 when at our busiest, we peaked at 310 calls per cay—almost twice as many people call us today for assistance with their pets or out of concern for other animals. The bad news is that you are right, our phone system is unable to handle the calls and 30 percent of you got a busy signal when you called. Be patient, we are adding three additional incoming lines and three new phone stations on the inside to better receive your calls. We hope this will ease the congestion.

The parking lot is a tough one. On a slow day, 137 people will come to the shelter but some of you will never even get into the parking lot because of the limited number of spaces. The gravel road to the west (11th Avenue) isn't an option because of frequent break-ins, and crossing Columbia Boulevard is a suicide run. We hope to begin the first phase of our new shelter construction with a parking lot in the front lawn. Less lawn, but 45 additional parking spaces (we currently have 22) will greatly improve our ability to serve you.

The long lines out the door are a reflection of the limited office space for adoptions and interest in our animals for adoption. We have four adoption staff on duty, but only three desks available. We would like to remodel the office but the truth is we have just outgrown our facility. The physical shelter is the most significant limiting factor in adoptions and our ability to serve the community."

Profile
ERNIE SWIGERT

Ernest Charles Swigert was a generous man, supporting a myriad of local institutions that included the Portland Art Museum, the Oregon Symphony, the Oregon Historical Society, the Portland Opera, the Haven Project, the Berry Botanic Garden and the Delta Society. But as a leading philanthropist here—scion of a prominent Portland family—Swigert was perhaps best known as a champion of the Oregon Humane Society. Swigert loved all animals, but doted especially on his own dogs. Wherever Swigert went, his pooches went—whether it was out to dinner in Portland or traveling to Europe. Pot, a toy poodle, and his two black Labs, Sherman and Beauregard, were at his side when he died at home at age 83 in 2008.

Swigert's concern for creatures led him to spearhead the capital campaign for the construction of the new OHS shelter in 1999. Swigert made sure that all the needed funds were raised before ground was broken. It is little wonder that the spacious, state-of-the-art Ernest C. Swigert Animal Shelter is considered a model for humane societies the world around.

Swigert was the son of Mr. and Mrs. E. G. Swigert, and the grandson of pioneering West Coast industrialist and engineer C. F. Swigert.

The Swigert family owned ESCO Corp., a steel-plating business that also produced earth-moving equipment. A spinoff company, Hyster, sold forklift trucks worldwide.

Young Ernest was educated at Hillside School, now Catlin Gabel Academy, before heading East for prep school at Milton Academy, followed by Harvard University. As a member of the U. S. Army's 754th Tank Battalion from 1944-46, he received a number of medals, including the Bronze Star. Swigert joined the family business after World War II, but left to find a new life in The Netherlands. Swigert spent 25 years on a converted barge, traveling the waterways of western Europe.

After he returned home to Portland, *Willamette Week* described Swigert as the city's "original party animal." Even at 75, the article noted, "He's slowed down a bit, but he can still throw a mean party at his West Hills pad." That home, not incidentally, is listed in the U.S. Register of Historic Places.

Swigert was such a beloved Portland figure that he was known affectionately as "Uncle Ernie." In a hand-written note to Uncle Ernie following an OHS luncheon, CEO Sharon Harmon wrote, "Our strength and understanding is due in no small part to your leadership and generosity."

In 2006, Harmon presented the organization's first Diamond Collar Lifetime Achievement Award to Swigert. She wrote upon his passing, "The Oregon Humane Society bears Ernie Swigert's name above our main entrance, a small testament to his incredible love of companion animals and the inspiration he provided to all of us here," Harmon said. "His spirit will always be here to inspire us."

From horse-drawn to horseless carriages: In 1947 OHS reported "On November 3rd, Wentworth & Irwin, 123 NE Oregon Street, distributors of GMC Trucks, will display, in their floor show, a new ambulance built to our specifications which will be put in service by us on November 8th. The body was designed by our employees. One of the interesting things about it is that it is one of the first vehicles in Portland to be equipped with the new Mobile Telephone Service. This is one of three trucks operated by us to be so equipped and means that emergency Police calls on injured animals can be relayed directly to one of our cars cruising the city."

Before 1972, OHS patrolled the streets to pick up strays (top left). Through the decades since, we've been on the road as emergency rescuers.

11

Across Oregon: Putting the "O" in OHS

"The society was never meant to be just a shelter. Your Oregon Humane Society is the leader of a region-wide network of animal welfare workers who advocate to make the Pacific Northwest the best place for all animals to live—including two-legged ones."

~ Dale Dunning, *OHS Magazine*, Summer 1995

Founder Thomas Lamb Eliot captured a fundamental aspect of the mission of OHS in 1895 when he noted that "many persons from neighboring counties and from all parts of the state write to us, asking attention to local abuses." While headquartered in Portland, the organization has always thought of its sphere of influence as what one early official called "the whole vast state of Oregon."

Portland personnel eagerly helped communities around Oregon establish their own animal welfare centers. Initially, these groups were known as "affiliates," but today each agency is entirely independent. Still, there has long been a tradition of cooperation and collaboration throughout the state. Records from 1940 show that emissaries from Polk County and Salem headed to Portland to report on the progress they were making up in setting up a joint Marion-Polk County society, and to request that someone from Portland come down to deliver a pep talk. Two emissaries from Bend stopped by the same year, also seeking guidance. The next year brought visitors from Klamath Falls. Midway through 1941, a Portland official traveled to Eugene to help finalize plans for a Lane County Humane Society, to be backed primarily by a group from the University of Oregon. By 1960, the guarantee of partnership with the Portland-based institution was codified with the following language and the stipulation that member-groups must pay the exorbitant annual fee of one dollar:

MERCY WORK WIDE

Letters Show What Humane Society Is Doing.

APPEAL FOR STATE AID

Bill Providing Appropriation of $3000 Unfavorably Reported.
W. T. Shannon Declares the Need Is Urgent.

PORTLAND, Feb. 12.—(To the Editor.) —In view of the fact that the bill introduced at the present session of the Oregon Legislature by the Oregon Humane Society, asking for a small appropriation of $ 00, to aid in humane work, was unfavorably reported upon, we desire to present a partial statement of the work which is being done by this society, and to show the great need of state aid.

The following letters are but a very small portion of the complaints that are being daily received from all parts of the state, and we would earnestly request that the ways and means committee would carefully examine these reports and reconsider their former decision, and realize the great necessity for appropriating the above amount in carrying on this indispensible work:

Baker City, Or., Feb. 10, 1909.—Gentlemen: Will you use your influence in securing legislation that will lessen some of the cruelties in the marking of livestock? There are owners in this county, owners of cattle, who cut one ear nearly off, close to the head, and allow it to hang by a small fragment. Nearly every one who sees them remarks of the cruelty, but no steps are taken to prevent the practice. Hoping that this message will not arrive too late, I remain, W. H. S.

Hood River, Or., Feb. 28, 1908.—I write to ask you if you please send me constitution and by-laws of the Humane So-

The article continues:

Springfield, Or., Jan. 21, 1908.—Dear Sir: Am interested in the work of the Oregon Humane Society. Any information which you may be pleased to furnish in regard to it will be thankfully received. H. G.

Jefferson, Or., Aug. 8, 1908.—Dear Sir: At the last meeting of the Woman's Club of Jefferson, we decided to put in a drinking fountain for horses at this place. Noticing that several have been erected at Portland through the efforts of your Humane Society, any information on this subject as to the cost of the fountains will be thankfully received. D. H. I.

Sherwood, Or., Sept. 10, 1908.—Dear Sir: Cruelty to animals in the country. Frequently we have noticed in the columns of the Journal where persons are fined for cruelty to animals. In the city it is easy to detect, but in the country, where on a farm a poor horse is worked hard every day, often over-burdened, notwithstanding the fact that the poor animal's feet are rotted and sore to a frightful state. Is there no protection in rural districts for the poor suffering animals? Many are the cases which come to my notice and need the attention of a humane officer, but it is not generally known by the farmer to whom a complaint should be sent. Will you kindly oblige by giving such information. A SUBSCRIBER.

Walla Walla, Wash., Aug. 10, 1908.—Dear Sir: Will you kindly inform me as to the proper method of procedure for securing the organization of a Humane Society for Walla Walla? I am very anxious to see some movement made toward checking the cruelty here toward horses and other animals. S. E.

Portland, Or., Sept. 12, 1908.—Dear Sir: I wish to thank you for the prompt attention you have given to the extreme case of cruelty I reported and for your letter in answer to mine. It is a great relief to know that there is some one to whom matters of cruelty can be reported and who will give careful attention to them. I have heard several people speak of the good work done by the Humane Society here, and I certainly appreciate the kind response I have had to the several cases I reported, and your society should certainly receive state aid. H. B. C.

McMinnville, Or., Nov. 13, 1908.—Dear Sir: I wish to call your attention to the manner in which they have of plucking turkies alive. The turkey is hung up by the feet, then a sharp iron hook, made for the purpose, is run through the lower jaw, with a heavy weight suspended, which holds the wretch from wriggling. Then it is picked clean. They die a natural death. Sometimes they walk around afterwards. Thanksgiving is near at hand and we would like to have you send an officer here and order that this barbarous practice may be stopped. M. M. I.

W. T. SHANAHAN.

Even in 1909, Oregonians statewide sought aid from OHS.

"Any duly organized society (incorporated or unincorporated) organized for the prevention of cruelty of every kind and in any form to human beings and to the lower order of animals and living creatures and maintaining its principal office in the state of Oregon, may become a member of the Oregon Humane Society as a perpetual member upon making application therefore on forms submitted by the Oregon Humane Society and the payment in January of each year an annual fee of only $1.00, and thereby will be entitled to the fullest assistance and cooperation of the Oregon Humane Society in carrying out its objectives."

This sense of cooperation moved the OHS board in 1964 to appropriate $10,000 "to further humane causes around the state, to acquaint people of Oregon with the ideals of the society and perhaps to organize new groups." OHS supporters took this task seriously, no matter how the effort was conducted. "Societies are not formed in a week, month or two months," wrote OHS Trustee Frances Blakely in 1965. "I find that continued correspondence, back and forth, is as effective as making expensive trips before there has been a concentration of interest shown by people in a community." Blakely also pointed out the American Humane Association was "intensely interested" in promoting these new groups.

Before a humane society had even been established in Josephine County, a representative from Portland drove down with crates of dog food to help out. There he encountered Miss Grace Hall, known around Grants Pass as "a one-woman humane society." The Portland delegate reported back that he was "astounded" by the work she had done, entirely at her own expense.

The time for these kinds of statewide efforts seemed to have arrived. Like water simmering before a hard boil, more branches began bubbling up. The Josephine County Humane Society was formed late in the summer of 1965, and almost immediately, OHS officials in Portland were fielding inquiries from John Day. A Salem group was ready to organize a society, and other groups were making plans in Gold Beach, Pendleton and Corvallis. Late in 1965, OHS in Portland paid the cost of filing incorporation papers for the new Marion County Humane Society, and even supplied the group its first block of membership cards. By early spring 1966, the fledgling Marion County Humane Society was investigating its first case of animal cruelty.

The wave of interest extended beyond new outposts. In notes from 1965, Frances Blakely commented on an increase in mail from people expressing concern about experiments on live animals, including cats and goats, in biology classes. The letters urged OHS to advocate for a new law prohibiting the use of live creatures for experiments in schools.

Visits from Portland continued, as new communities expressed interest. There was a trip to the Jackson County Humane Society on Table Rock Road in rural Medford in 1967, the same year that officials from OHS in Portland were invited to speak at the annual banquet of the Josephine County Humane Society. The following year, a team from Portland was off to Salem to help set up the Willamette Valley Humane Society. A quasi-rival group calling itself "Federated Humane Societies (Oregon)" popped up in 1974. OHS diplomatically pointed out that membership in other related animal welfare agencies would not disqualify any group from affiliate membership in the Oregon Humane Society.

Profile
FRANCES BLAKELY

It was Christmas time, and she needed a job. When a young, brash Frances Whitehead spotted a notice in *The Baker Herald* seeking someone to sell advertising, she marched right into the newspaper office and presented herself as just the person for the job, despite the fact that she had never sold an ad in her life.

"They must have liked my Southern accent," the Kentucky native said years later. But instead of assigning her to the advertising department, they turned her into a news woman. She worked as a reporter at *The Herald*, and then rose to city editor. A year and a half later she moved to the *Portland Telegram*, and later to the *Oregon Journal*.

Reporters are often thought of as hard-boiled and tough, but Frances Blakely—as she came to be known after her 1923 marriage to Ralph Waldo Blakely—had a soft spot. During her nearly 20 years at the *Journal*, Blakely frequently used her talents as a feature writer to help find homes for abandoned animals. She also became, as her 1983 obituary in *The Oregonian* put it, "a mainstay" at the Oregon Humane Society. The newspaper noted that she served on the OHS Board of Trustees for 30 years, and was the organization's secretary for more than 50 years.

Blakely carried out that job with characteristic fierceness. For instance, she took issue with a certain set of minutes that had been submitted under her name:

"Although signed on typewriter by 'Frances Blakely,' these minutes are not my minutes and have been rearranged by someone else."

How and why she came West from Kentucky is lost to mystery. One legend has that she was married off in her home state at age 14. By the time of the 1920 census, she was divorced and living in Oregon. After marrying, she and Ralph Waldo Blakely lived on NE Grant Place, a neighborhood that retains its charm to this day.

In the unliberated 1920s, women were still proud to go by their husbands' names. "Mrs. Ralph Blakely" is listed as an OHS board member in the 1920s, and was tapped as Acting Secretary in 1932. The following year she was elected Secretary. Throughout her years at OHS, she was instrumental in helping communities around Oregon to establish independent shelters and animal protection groups. In 1940, she reported first on a visit to Marion and Polk counties, and soon enough the same year, on the establishment of a humane society there. After Blakely spoke at a public meeting at the Salem Chamber of Commerce, the new society presented her with a lifetime membership.

Her efforts to spread the OHS spirit continued. In 1940, she met with a delegate from Bend who wanted to start an animal welfare group there. The following year it was Jackson County and then Lane County.

Early in 1965, Blakely briefly became a paid employee of OHS, but she quickly opted to return on a volunteer basis. Her focus continued to be on building a network of humane societies throughout the state. "I will continue to look for other communities that are interested in organizing societies," she said. "Societies are not formed in a week, month or two months and I find that continued correspondence, back and forth, is as effective as making expensive trips before there has been a concentration of interest shown by people in a community."

As devoted as she was to OHS, Blakely also had a private side. She owned homestead property in Christmas Valley, where this strong, independent woman built all her own furniture. Blakely also had land near Troutdale overlooking the Columbia and Sandy Rivers, where she buried many dogs and cats in a private pet cemetery.

When she died at 94, family suggested that donations in her memory be made—of course—to the Oregon Humane Society.

LANGUAGE & TERMINOLOGY

The words we use reflect our changing attitudes through the years: in the 19th century we spoke of "dumb animals" and "brute creation." By 1940, we saw ourselves as a place of refuge, calling the newly rebuilt OHS shelter an "Animal Harbour" with a "Cat Haven" to house homeless felines. In 2001, language was changing again to a "kinder and gentler" animal vocabulary espoused in this article in the Winter *OHS Magazine*.

a·chānge·in (lán-guage)

How things are said, what words are used for descriptions, affect perception.
Here are some kinder and gentler terms to incorporate in your animal vocabulary:

Guardian rather than owner.

Homeless not stray or unwanted.

House·training instead of housebreaking.

Positive·reinforcement rather than obedience training.

Free-roaming·cat not a wild, feral cat.

Companion·animal in place of pet.

Adopt not buy.

And so the proliferation continued: The Evergreen-Doe Humane Society started in McMinnville in 1975, dedicating its sparkling new shelter five years later. As these regional offices took hold, OHS provided ongoing support. When OHS discovered in 1992 that a new animal shelter for Columbia County was only designed to maintain a temperature of 55 degrees, OHS stepped in assure adequate temperature control for the animal residents. Columbia County also asked Portland to write in opposition to a new ordinance in Albany allowing residents to use bows, crossbows and air guns to kill nutria. When the Josephine County Humane Society was found to be overcrowded with sick animals that same year, the OHS board explored options to help.

Today's Oregon Humane Society continues to provide animal care assistance to smaller shelters around the state. In Medford, for instance, Jackson County commissioners invited OHS in 2012 to audit their shelter and increase the percentage of animals they saved. OHS veteran Autumn White conducted a comprehensive audit that reviewed policies and procedures and examined key programs essential to optimizing the live release rate. White worked side-by-side with the Medford shelter staff and volunteers, and together they were able to greatly increase the save rates at Medford.

12

Fountains and Sculptures and Orcas, Oh My!

These days, fountains in Portland are celebrated for their beauty.

But when the city was new, OHS just wanted to make sure thirsty draft animals had plenty to drink. As Simon Benson provided Portland's famous "bubblers" for humans, so did the Oregon Humane Society work to ensure that horses, dogs and other animals had ready access to water as they hauled the loads that built and supplied our town.

Portland's Elk Fountain on SW Main Street is an urban landmark. With its powerful antlers and prominent perch, the statue was a gift to the city in 1900 from former Mayor David Thompson, honoring OHS. Thompson, then president of the Oregon Humane Society, had the statue placed in the middle of the road so that draft animals could easily slake their thirst. Soon after the stag took his post atop its sturdy pedestal, a local artist said that for only $30, he could wire the antlers with electric light bulbs. The offer was politely declined.

In the summer of 1906, July was swelteringly hot in Portland. Humans were suffering, and so were animals. OHS Secretary William Shanahan wrote to *The Oregonian*, beseeching the city to help horses parched with thirst in the dreadful heat. For years, OHS had agitated for improved hydration for the animals who pulled heavy loads throughout the city and up the steep hills of Portland. Shanahan noted that "our city of nearly 200,000 souls, covering more than 40 square miles, contains less than 10 fountains and but two of these on the West side of the river, where man and beast can drink." Such installations need not be expensive, Shanahan insisted, and indeed, designs were available at OHS. "Wealthy and benevolent citizens," he urged, should "start this important work and let it be said that Portland is not only the 'Rose City' but is also a city of fountains."

Pacific Parade

Sunday Journal

PORTLAND, OREGON, DECEMBER 12, 1948

Years Pass, But Service Still Free See Page Three

Dedicated in 1907, this Ensign Fountain was moved to the OHS Cemetery around 1918.

In the spring of 1907, Shanahan's repeated pleas were answered when The National Humane Alliance contacted OHS about donating a fountain. Shanahan moved quickly to secure the donation. Hermon Lee Ensign of New York City, founder of the National Humane Alliance, had amassed a large fortune as a telegrapher, journalist, advertising manager and writer. But his passion remained the ethical treatment of animals. The fountain presented to the City of Portland in 1907 was one of more than 100 that he gave to communities across America between 1903 and 1913. The large granite fountain was shipped to Portland from Vinalhaven, Maine, and soon became a functional urban monument. A photo and caption in *The Oregonian* from September 13, 1908, depicted a "Handsome Drinking Fountain at Sixth and Ankeny."

Originally slated for installation at Sixth Avenue and West Burnside Street, the fountain instead found a home a block south at Sixth Avenue and SW Ankeny Street. Within the year, traffic there had increased by 50 percent, and "all day drivers of teams may be seen watering their horses at the fountain." A "diminutive donkey," as the newspaper recounted, had stopped for a drink after a hard day of pulling an advertising cart announcing, among other things, a "BIG SHOE SALE."

Portland's Ensign Fountain drew steady traffic, but even so, did not remain at Sixth and Ankeny for long. Around 1919, as cars and trucks took over from horses and buggies and roughly the same time as the construction of the OHS Animal Cemetery, the fountain was moved to the grounds of the Humane Society. The fountain is as massive as it is architecturally distinctive. It weighs five tons and stands six feet tall, a column of solid granite with a large bowl about four feet off the ground—the perfect drinking height for horses. Around the base sit four smaller bowls. A brass plaque honors Ensign for his gift.

By 1965, donkeys no longer plied Portland's streets, and the old fountain had sprung some serious leaks. As is so often the collaborative tradition among Portland nonprofits, one OHS turned to another. The Humane Society's Frances Blakely remembered that former Oregon Historical Society president George Hines had also been one of the organizers of the humane society. Hines had passed away in 1940 at age 95, but Blakely reasoned that Hines, of all people, might have kept records that would aid in its repairs. One board member suggested turning the leaky fountain into a flower planter. Harumph, sniffed another member of the board, Mr. Henderson. Henderson declared he was "not of the school for making hats out of lamp shades or flower pots out of fountains." Henderson moved instead that the board seek an estimate for installing a new circulation system in the poor old fountain. Motion granted.

In 2007, a century after its original installation, the fountain was again restored, thanks to the generosity of longtime OHS supporter Jamie St. Mark. Designers of the new Animal Medical Learning Center had planned to move the fountain, but it was so firmly planted that an attempt to dislodge it from its current location with a commercial crane only resulted in the crane itself tilting over without budging the fountain. So the Ensign-St. Mark Fountain remains on our memorial grounds, a reminder of earlier generations' commitment to ensuring that animals had plenty of water to drink.

For almost half a century, the Olds Fountain provided liquid relief for fire horses, animals drawing heavy loads, dogs, cats and birds. The firefighters loved the water source that stood on a parking strip between NE Union and Grand Streets, and they helped local residents with its upkeep until the late 1940s. But in 1949, a feud broke out over ownership. Sadly for OHS, its proof of ownership of the fountain had

Portland firefighters rallied to ensure that the Olds Fountain could find its way to the grounds of OHS.

been lost to the devastating fire that burned down its first shelter on Columbia Boulevard. The City of Portland countered that legally, it owned the fountain because it was on city land. An article in the *Oregon Journal* brought out the collectors and antique dealers, ready to make top-dollar offers.

One day, 13 firefighters asked OHS president Harvey Wells what he would do with the fountain if he could prove ownership. Wells promised the firefighters that he would see it painted, repaired and put to use—if not in its current location, then on the grounds of the Oregon Humane Society. Wells lit up in a smile, but asked no questions when he was presented with a plaque that someone had quietly removed. "Presented to the Oregon Humane Society by Mrs. W. P. Olds, 1907," the plaque read. The Olds Fountain was moved to OHS grounds, where it remains to this day.

When Homer Angell decided to retire in 1964, after more than a third of a century of service to OHS as a trustee, he and his wife Mary thought they'd make a special donation to the organization that had meant so much to them. The Angells' check for $1,000 was used to purchase a sculpture by Tom Hardy of two playful dogs. Those two pups are still cavorting in the OHS Memorial Gardens.

Best known for his photographs of Weimeraners in all manner of costumes and poses, William Wegman is also a sculptor. In 2001, Portland's Pearl Arts Foundation commissioned Wegman to create a piece of art for the North Park Blocks, near the old Customs House. Wegman came up with a piece called Dog Bowl, a cast-bronze dog bowl that sits on a checkerboard designed to resemble old-fashioned kitchen floor tile. Wegman told the arts aficionados assembled for the installation that the sculpture was "for dogs, not for people," and

that he preferred not to think of it as public art. Wegman then vowed to donate some of the earnings from the installation to OHS—and sure enough, the following year, he fulfilled his promise.

And then there was Ethelbert, the hapless orca who took a wrong turn and ended up stranded in the Columbia Slough, more than 100 miles upstream from the sea. The young killer whale caused such a sensation as he splashed around in the Slough that he achieved a kind of mythic status.

Tom Hardy's frolicking dogs honor the "zeal and devotion" of Homer D. Angell. Tom McCall can be seen in the background.

A WHALE OF A TALE

In the fall of 1931, spectators marveled at the enormous, black-and-white creature leaping around in the Columbia Slough. Was it a giant sturgeon? A blackfish? Possibly a porpoise? Some unidentified beast from the bottom of the sea? A Northwest cousin of the Loch Ness monster?

Soon enough, the animal cavorting in the Columbia was identified as a young orca. Naturalists surmised that it had followed the salmon run up the Columbia before becoming trapped in the Slough. The 15-foot-long mammal attracted a kind of local fan club. *The Oregonian* newspaper wanted to name it "Jimmy McCool's Whale," after its own wildlife writer. But public sentiment prevailed and the whale was unofficially christened Ethelbert.

While families gasped in wonderment at Ethelbert's playful antics, sportsmen armed with rifles considered how to snare him. Hunting laws at the time specified bag limits for deer, elk, antelope and even forbade using firearms to take fish. But as a marine mammal, Ethelbert was, so to speak, neither fish nor fowl. More than a few shots were fired before Gov. Julius L. Meier ordered a halt to such behavior. Sadly, Ethelbert's wounds became infected before anyone could come to his rescue.

OHS convened an emergency board meeting to discuss what should be done with—or for—Ethelbert. Bryan Allison, former chief engineer for the Pacific-American Whaling Company, told the board that the orca was, basically, stuck—able neither to go farther up the river nor to return to the Pacific. Allison said the animal could not obtain the right sort of food, and moreover, was covered by fungus. This was a killer whale, he pointed out, so a rescue mission would be risky. He advised disposal.

At the same meeting, the OHS board voted not to join forces with the managers of Jantzen Beach, who had sought permission to catch the whale in a net and then transfer it to a large saltwater tank for public display. "The Society has always opposed the exploitation of any animal," the board declared. Under Allison's guidance, the society advised swift disposal of Ethelbert "in a humane manner and as soon as possible."

But before nature, or OHS, could take its course, an old-time whaler named Edward O. Lessard and his son stepped in to settle the matter. In a chartered boat, the father and son, Joe T. Lessard, approached Ethelbert—and quickly harpooned him.

"It was the quickest killing I ever made," the elder Lessard boasted. "Usually it takes half a day or a day to kill a whale. This one was dead as a doornail in less than five minutes."

Lessard promptly announced that he would place Ethelbert on exhibition. Just as swiftly, OHS said it would seek the Lessards' arrest on grounds of disturbing the public peace and morals, killing a fish with illegal tackle and fishing in the slough with illegal tackle. The society noted that it had urged death for the whale as an act of mercy, not at the hands of a rapacious whaler. But the charges did not stick. No laws about inland whaling existed.

(Continued on next page)

(Continued from previous page)

While Lessard was trying to figure out how to retrieve Ethelbert from the bottom of the Slough, a representative from the Portland Chemical Company showed up, offering to finance the whale's embalmment for public display if the proceeds could be sent to the Community Chest.

"Nix," said Lessard. "It's my dead whale."

A nasty, eight-year court battle ensued until finally the state caved, questioning the value of arguing over a dead whale.
The Lessards were allowed to take possession of Ethelbert if they paid $103 in court fees.

Accounts differ about what finally happened to Ethelbert. Some say that Ed Lessard carted him around in a metal box, as a kind of traveling dead whale carnival show. The Lessards, who by then had moved to St. Helens, were said to have buried Ethelbert on another of their properties near Washougal, Wash.

But the dead do not always rest easy. Poor Ethelbert. In 1949, reports began to circulate about a strange smell emanating from a piece of land near St. Helens. Sure enough, there was Ethelbert, inside a rusted metal box. Soon after, the beleaguered orca was properly buried, far deeper than where the Lessards had left him.

Ethelbert, Portland's Famous Whale, Gives 8000 Spectators Real Thrills

Ethelbert, the elongated whale which has been holding open house in Oregon slough since Monday, took first place yesterday in Portland as a drawing card when more than 8000 persons lined the banks to watch his leisurely cavorting.

As an individual attraction, Ethelbert has been bested in Portland in the matter of drawing crowds only by Jack Dempsey, Queen Marie, Colonel Lindbergh and a few other celebrities.

It took three score football players from two colleges, another score of handlers and coaches, and two big bands—all dressed up in fancy uniforms—to outdraw Ethelbert yesterday in Portland

What would the promoters give to fence Oregon slough and keep Ethelbert there forever?

Anyway, if Ethelbert doesn't yield to the yearning for the sea whence he came, there'll be 10,000 persons, at least, out to see him today, rivermen predict.

No touchdowns or spectacular runs were made yesterday in Oregon slough, but Ethelbert packed the banks just the same. There was no music, no song and dance acts, no gags, but it was a good show.

There probably wasn't one person in the 8000 whose pulse didn't quicken when Ethelbert pushed his snout up

to the top of the water, snorted like a horse fed on green oats, and blew a jet of dirty water and vapor into the air.

"Thar she blows!" shouted those on the bank. And in every group of spectators—fascinated through the afternoon by the game of wondering where Ethelbert would come up next—excitement brought out exclamations of surprise and wonder. When Ethelbert contemptuously shoved his dorsal fin up out of the water the "ohs" and "ahs" rippled down the bank.

It required a dozen deputy sheriffs and traffic officers to handle the streams of automobiles in the vicinity of the Interstate bridge, where James McCool's whale is furnishing Portlanders with the newest thing in outdoor entertainment.

Cars partly filled the big parking place south of Oregon slough, where there is room enough for 3500, while Jantzen Beach amusement park on the other side of Ethelbert's playground was open for additional machines.

Respecting the wishes of his public, Ethelbert went through his complete routine of tricks.

Now he has this routine down so well that those who have watched him for several days know just about what

Concluded on Page 6, Column 1

Ethelbert was the biggest crowd-pleaser in town, according to this
October 18, 1931, front page article in *The Sunday Oregonian*.

13

Teach Your Children Well

"Humane education is the perfect way to teach the Golden Rule through pets. Kind empathetic children mature into kind, empathetic adults."

~ Norma Paulus, Oregon Superintendent of Public Instruction 1990-99.

Its commitment to humane education is surely among the reasons that OHS has not just survived, but has prospered and grown with each successive generation. This dedication dates back to the organization's earliest days. Indeed, the founders of OHS valued humane education as the ultimate solution to human cruelty in all forms. "I may say to the children of the schools and city that we count upon you as our chief allies in cultivating a spirit of kindness to all dumb creatures," OHS President Thomas Lamb Eliot declared in his 1888 OHS anniversary meeting. At the same celebration, "200 little children stood up and sang a song, clapping and swinging their hands for elocutionary effect." Prize-winning essays were honored, including those written by Walter Holman and Julius Meier, both students at Park School.

HUMANE EDUCATION REGARDED AS HELPFUL IN DEVELOPMENT OF CHARACTER OF CHILD

Gentleness, Mercy and Reverence for Life Are Power Behind World Movement to Protect Animals and Human Beings From Cruelty, Which Grows Stronger as Time Passes.

This is the second of a series of articles for use in connection with humane education in the school and home. It is now required by law that Oregon schools devote a "brief period each week to humane education, but such instruction is generally omitted, as teachers have found it difficult to obtain an outline of study. The present series has been prepared to meet this need by Jessie Hodge Millard, head of the children's department of the Portland public library, and Elpha K. Smith, a teacher in Portland public schools.

—H. W. LONGFELLOW.

How can I teach your children gentleness
And mercy to the weak and reverence for life,
When by your laws, your actions and your speech
You contradict the very things I teach?

A TEACHER made a remark last week which might apply to many who do not know about humane societies. She said: "I know nothing about humane societies, or what they do, and how can I teach humane education in my class? I sincerely want to do it, but I know so little about the subject. How did humane societies start?"

Acting on the suggestion, this article might enlighten those who do not know.

Societies for the prevention of cruelty to animals and societies for the prevention of cruelty to children sprang into existence to meet a special need. They have continued to exist and grow because they have done a work most efficiently which commands recognition and respect of the best thinking people in every community.

Probably we owe the first law in the world to prevent cruelty to animals to an Irish member of the British parliament. At one time, however, before this, the celebrated Lord Erskine tried to get such a law passed, but people made so much fun of him that he backed out and gave it up.

The story tells us that there came into the house of commons one day an Irish gentleman from Galway, or, as he was more familiarly known, "Dick" Martin. Well, Dick was noted for two things—he was very fond of animals and was known to be a fighter when he thought anyone insulted him.

The day he brought in his law to protect animals someone in the audience made a cat-call. Mr. Martin quickly stepped out into the middle of the floor of the house of commons and said, "I will be very much obliged for the name of the gentleman who has seen fit to insult me." The gentleman did not give his name and silence reigned supreme; amid great cheers Dick Martin walked back to his seat and his law became the law of Great Britain and the first law of its kind in the world.

There is one society in England to protect animals, composed of boys and girls, which has a membership of 50,000.

In 1866 the work for the prevention of cruelty to animals was started in the United States under the direction of Henry Bergh. During his stay in Russia he witnessed many cases of cruel treatment to animals and often interfered at the risk of his own life. On his way home he stopped in London and learned there about the Royal Society for the Prevention of Cruelty to Animals. Then and there he immediately decided to form a society in the United States. The newspapers aided him greatly by publishing his lectures in all the large cities and the public soon became interested. In April, 1866, the American Society for the Prevention of Cruelty to Animals was incorporated in the state of New York, the first society of its kind in the United States. William O. Stillman is now the president of the American Humane association at Albany, N. Y.

The humane societies of the world are performing a great service to humanity and all should join forces and unite to make them even better and of more value to the coming generations. The humane educational movement is certainly a broad one, reaching from humane treatment of animals on the one hand to peace with all nations on the other. Human and humane movements are thus closely related.

Humane education is fast coming to be regarded as obligatory and not voluntary in the public schools. In 19 of our states laws have been passed compelling humane education. They are: Colorado, North Dakota, Wyoming, Michigan, Texas, California, Oregon, Alabama, Oklahoma, Connecticut, Kentucky, Washington, New Hampshire, Massachusetts, Wisconsin, Maine, Pennsylvania, New York and Illinois.

Someone has said, "The lack of this education is the principal cause of crime." If this be true, how quickly, then, would vice and crime diminish, if the combined influence of the home, church and school would promote more kindness in the life of a child. Just what is humane education? Is it not the fostering in a child's mind those principles of justice, fair play and kindness toward every form of human and sub-human life capable of suffering?

The object should be to stop all forms of cruelty to human beings and the lower animals. The educational value, however, lies principally in its contribution to the broadening of the interest and sympathies of the child. Those who have given the matter much thought will agree that no subject is of greater importance in the formation of character, or in determining good citizenship for the future of the state, than humane education.

"Show me the laws of a state for the prevention of cruelty to animals, and I, in turn, will give you a correct estimate of the refinement, enlightenment, integrity and equity of that commonwealth's people," said L. T. Dashiell, who was at one time speaker from Texas in the house of representatives.

To the teachers: Inform yourself thoroughly on the subject of humane education if you expect to teach it successfully. You say you have no material and you do not know how to get it. The work is very simple. The office of the Oregon Humane society at the courthouse room 153, will give you all the information you desire. Use your own public library for books and material.

There are many books on the subject of the humane movement. A few are given here for those particularly interested, and you will find them in the adult department of the public library and its branches:

Coffin, "Appeal Against Slaughter"; McCrea, "Humane Movement"; Martinengo-Cesaresco, "Place of Animals in Human Thought"; Marvin, "Christ Among the Cattle"; Moore, "New Ethics"; Rowley, "Humane Idea"; Salt, "Animals' Rights"; Salt, "Killing for Sport"; Trine, "Every Living Creature"; Trist, "Under Dog."

"Humane societies of the world are performing a great service to humanity," read this 1921 *Oregonian* article.

Profile
GENERATIONS OF COMPASSION: THE MEIER FAMILY

Within families, the love of animals often passes among generations. So it was, certainly, with the Meier family of Portland. OHS was only 20 years old when a young boy at Park School named Julius Meier won the 1888 children's essay contest. Julius' essay launched a generations-long friendship between the Meier family and OHS. Julius, the younger son of Meier & Frank department stores founder Aaron Meier, joined the OHS Advisory Board as early as 1915. (Among his fellow board members was the well-known champion of women's rights, Abigail Scott Duniway.) OHS records show that in 1922, Julius and the family department store were both listed as life members of the society. A noted philanthropist, Meier also provided financial support to the Zionist Society of Oregon, the Lewis and Clark Exposition, the construction of the new Temple Beth Israel in 1927, and to many other causes that reflected his civic involvement. In 1930, Meier was handily elected governor, running as an independent. A year later, Gov. Meier ordered a stop to gunmen lining the banks of the Columbia who were taking pot-shots at a stranded orca whale the public had named "Ethelbert."

As with many prominent Oregon families, Meier passed his love of animals to subsequent generations. In the 1960s, Meier & Frank stores proudly displayed OHS poster contest winners. In 1964, Meier & Frank stores in downtown Portland, Salem and at the Lloyd Center displayed the animal-themed works of 300 young artists. The Oregon-based department store also sponsored the popular Mutt Show. By the 1990s, two more generations were helping the animals when Julius' great-nephew Roger Meier and his daughters Jill Garvey and Alix Goodman served on the steering committee for the shelter capital campaign. Today, Roger's widow Laura Meier and their daughters continue the Meier family's tradition of community philanthropy and help for the animals.

Field trips to OHS were a big hit with schoolchildren in the 1950s

This sense of civic awareness about animal welfare was by no means peculiar to Portland. Across the country in those early years, children organized into "Bands of Mercy," with publications and activities designed to instill the values of compassion, respect and kindness that remain at the heart of OHS humane education efforts to this day.

But OHS, not surprisingly, made a point of helping other communities make humane education a priority as they established their own humane societies. The OHS manual from 1915 quotes John L. Stoddard as saying, "We must place our hopes for the betterment of this world largely upon the rising generation. It is chiefly a matter of education. Enlist the sympathy of children in behalf of animals and half the battle is won and their future character determined."

John Gill, a prominent Portland businessman and OHS board member, spearheaded the first effort to pass a law addressing humane education for Oregon's children. Oregon Revised Statute 336. 067(1)(c) took effect in 1921, requiring students to receive one quarter hour of instruction in the humane treatment of animals each week. The state legislature eliminated the law in 1957, but OHS continued to emphasize humane education. People who grew up around Portland share fond memories of visits to the shelter and classroom visits from OHS humane educators and their dogs. With data that document the link between animal cruelty and violence against humans, two full-time educators continue the tradition today. Experiential learning and modern technology help them to convey what has always been an unwavering OHS tenet: Teaching children empathy for those less powerful will create the compassionate adults of tomorrow.

Older residents of Portland also will remember the daily broadcasts of Miss Hazel Kenyon, the director of radio for Portland public schools. Miss Kenyon created short stories out of press releases and announcements prepared at OHS. Every Monday, a radio artist named Mrs. Marion Lamb delivered a 15-minute broadcast called "Animal Antics," with the script provided by OHS. Both programs were heard over KPBS, using the same frequency as KXL.

And then there was *A Home for Butch*. More than likely, most Portland students from the 1940s-1960s saw this OHS film about a wayward mutt's picaresque odyssey from abandonment to a happy home and a forever family. The film was shown over and over until finally it was in shreds and could not be shown again. Fortunately, subsequent advances in technology made it possible to preserve this classic parable.

In 1924, OHS accomplished a "crowning achievement" when humane education became a required course of study in Oregon public schools.

TRUSTEES
W. C. Alderson,
    School Supt. Multnomah County
Mrs. Ralph W. Blakely
Pierre Baldwin
Charles G. Benson
Vivian Cooley
W. A. Dickson
Florence Holman
Col. E. Hofer
J. P. Kavanaugh
W. A. McDougall
Mrs. Edward Preble
David L. Piper
W. S. Raker
Gordon Soule
Mrs. F. W. Swanton
Mrs. Millie Trumbull
Mrs. L. D. Thomas

Sherry G. Charette, Business Secretary

Charles G. Benson, Attorney

GENERAL MANAGER
Mrs. F. W. Swanton

OFFICERS
President, Col. E. Hofer
Vice-President, W. S. Raker
Secretary, Vivian Cooley
Treasurer, Charles G. Benson
Corresponding Sec'y, F. F. Smith

ADVISORY BOARD
Geo. L. Baker, Mayor of Portland
Dr. T. L. Elliott, Portland
E. B. Piper, Portland
B. F. Irvine, Portland
Fred Boalt, Portland
Wm. Hanley, Burns
Dr. E. H. French, Medford
Dana S. Caufield, Oregon City
Sgt. E. L. Crate

Dr. A. G. Smith, Veterinarian

A. L. Cross, State Officer
W. A. Leach, City Officer
C. Robert Wade, Field Officer
James B. MacLaren,
    Supt. of City Pound and Refuge Home

Oregon Humane Society

153 COURT HOUSE

REFUGE AND POUND 535 COLUMBIA BLVD.
PHONE WALNUT 0764

MAIN OFFICE
MAIN 0378

PORTLAND, OREGON,

October 17, 1924

My Dear Humanitarian:

Finally, after three years of effort, the Oregon Humane Society have accomplished what we think is our crowning achievement,- made Humane Education a part of the course of study in every grade in every public school in Oregon. The law requires that it be taught one-half hour each week.

The State Superintendent of Public Instruction, J. A. Churchill, has just published a course of study for each grade, from first year to and including 8th year, a copy of which is enclosed. A High School course of study is yet to be arranged.

Senator John Gill, a member of the Humane Society and a senior member of the firm of J. K. Gill & Co., Booksellers, is the author of the law. Credit for its becoming a law is largely due to the cooperation of our General Manager, Mrs. F. W. Swanton with the Senator. They contend and rightly, too, that if a child has eight years of Humane education, along lines indicated in this course of study, that when he shall have finished school he will be a live, active, Humanitarian, with a greater ambition to aid and befriend his HUMAN fellows, as well as other creatures of the earth and air and the societies for the prevention of cruelty to animals will devote their time to more constructive work than police duty.

If this law could be duplicated in every State in the Union - and it should be - every man, woman and child would be a self-appointed Humane officer.

Show the sample course of study to your teacher, your legislator and your Humane Society and then follow our example. It is not copyrighted.

Humanely yours,

W. S. Raker

W. S. RAKER, Vice President

P.S. "Be kind to animals. You are one yourself."

Profile

CAROL SHIVELEY: TEACHER'S PETS

Ten years after taking over the OHS Humane Education program, Carol Shiveley, third from left, clowned with summer campers in 1999.

In 1989, the newly-hired summer camp director quit after just two weeks on the job. That was when Carol Shiveley stepped in, jumping at the chance to run two camps, five days each for third and fourth graders and fifth and sixth graders. "*I love kids and animals. It was a perfect fit,*" Shiveley said. A year later, OHS Executive Director Dale Dunning asked her to write a plan for humane education. Again, it was a dream assignment for Carol. She started clubs and camps, visited schools, and launched the poster contest full tilt.

At first, Carol's job consisted of directing the education program and administering the pet therapy program. Volunteers took shelter animals to rest homes, hospitals, and clubs. Carol matched teams to facilities, cultivating relationships with activity directors. She provided potluck education seminars for pet partners to share their experiences, and ordered jackets for dogs to wear while on duty. Over the next two and a half years, the education and pet therapy programs grew so large that Director Dunning made her choose between the two. She chose the education program, but noted that when she left, there were 120 volunteers with pets in the therapy program. Carol was officially designated OHS Education Director in 1992 and worked 21 years in the program that married her passions for working with children and animals.

Tuxedo, the coal-black terrier with wiry hair and a white blaze that Carol adopted, reminded people of a penguin. She took him everywhere. "*Tux was a foolproof dog and he excelled at working with very sick kids,*" she said. Tux even served as ring bearer for a wedding ceremony at the OHS rose garden. In recognition of his philanthropic contributions, Tuxedo's paw prints were showcased at the Oregon Zoo.

In developing humane education programs for kids, Carol focused on the importance of spaying and neutering pets. "We turned around a generation by messaging the benefits of spay and neutering pets," she said. During her 21-year tenure as director of humane education at OHS, Carol estimates she saw half a million kids. These young people may have learned a great deal, but Carol considers herself the real winner "Education can change lives, but I got so many benefits," she said, adding that she feels blessed that she could grow a generation of kids by instilling humane education.

The Association of Professional Humane Educators (APHE) started in Oregon, with Carol as its first president. APHE is now a national organization and Carol, now retired, is a lifetime member.

Poster Contest

In 1948, OHS launched a poster and essay contest that continues to reach thousands of students throughout the state. To ensure that the competition does not simply produce endless drawings of "My Dog Spot," OHS provides themes appropriate to each grade level, such as "Be Kind and Love Your Pet," or "Everyone Can Do Something To Help Homeless Pets." Poster winners and their families, teachers and friends are honored at the OHS "A-cat-emy Awards." In pre-Internet days, winning posters were on view at department stores, the Multnomah County Central Library, the Portland Art Museum and other popular gathering spots. Today, winning entries may be viewed at *oregonehumane.org/services/student-programs/poster-story-contest.*

This 2004 winning poster was created by first-grader Savannah Harris of Bridlemile Elementary.

Poster contest winners on display at the downtown Meier & Frank Building.

Thaovi Duong of Reynolds High School was the 11th grade winner in 2011.

A new century brought renewed focus on education, including OHS in-school presentations, summer camp and after-school clubs and community service programs that include hands-on opportunities to work with shelter pets. In 2000, OHS reached more than 24,000 adults and children with humane education activites. The OHS Summer Camp experience, first offered in 1986, offers day campers informative and entertaining activities. Here's what a typical day looked like for 2016 OHS summer campers:

What Campers Do: Sample Day Schedule, 2016

A typical day at OHS summer camp includes a morning, mid-day and an afternoon session. For example: morning presentations; mid-day animal time, a craft, and lunch; one afternoon presentation and a game. Presentations cover a variety of animal and shelter-related topics and often include visits from animals.

Here's how the day looks:

9:30 - 10am	*Animal Story/Video & Small Animal Garden Time*
10 - 10:45am	*Humane Investigations Presentation*
10:45 - 11am	*Break*
11am - 12pm	*Rabbits Just Like Us Presentation*
12 - 2pm	*Rotate through four activities—30 minutes each with shelter dogs, cats/small animals, lunch, crafts*
2 - 2:45pm	*Shelter Medicine Presentation*
2:45 - 3pm	*Snack*
3 - 3:15pm	*Group Picture*
3:15 - 3:45pm	*Game*
3:45 - 4pm	*Clean-up and Goodbye*

Running for eight one-week sessions each year, OHS summer camp also allows young people, grades three through 12, to explore animal-related careers. Visits from animals are not just limited to dogs and cats. These campers hang out with goats, llamas, miniature horses—even boa constrictors. A lottery system assures that that coveted camp spots are assigned fairly. Scholarships funded by OHS donors allow campers who cannot afford full tuition to take part.

After a full day of stimulating activities, OHS summer campers go home happy and exhausted.

Who doesn't want to hang out with a well-dressed alpaca? These OHS summer campers are all smiles enjoying a visit with their new four-legged friend.

14

Foster Care

Whether delivered through official channels or provided on an ad hoc basis, foster care for animals has been around for many years. With the goal of providing care for animals who were not yet ready for adoption, people have taken dogs, cats and other creatures home for a little TLC in a non-institutional setting. Foster families must adjust to animals who may be skittish, hyper-energetic, fearful or unpredictable. In turn these animals learn to live around non-abusive, caring humans who set reasonable limits on pet behavior, and who reward good performance with praise, affection and, often, edible goodies.

For years there was no official census on foster care in placements. Now known as Outpatient Services, OHS operates a tightly run program involving hundreds of foster homes and thousands of foster pets. These compassionate families give foster animals another chance at placement into permanent homes. These pets may be too young to be spayed or neutered. Some are recovering from abuse, injury or illness. Others have suffered from over-stress in the shelter environment, sometimes shutting down into a kind of creature catatonia known as shelter shock. As records began to be kept, OHS knew that by 1997, more than 100 foster families were caring for 150 animals on any day. Of these, more than 90 percent were adopted into forever homes.

"This year we are doing things differently in that were are using our 120 foster families not just for newborns, pregnant cats, or recuperating dogs, but when we run out of room." "Our foster families directly saved the lives of 1,200 animals in 1998 alone."

~ *OHS Magazine*, Fall 1999

Former foster care coordinator Kelly Podoloff offers a smiling welcome to an energetic litter of kittens who havve just returned from time well-spent in a loving foster family.

Profile
TANYA ROBERTS

People on the brink of surrendering a pet are often frantic, notes Tanya Roberts, who leads the OHS training and behavior department: "Maybe they've let a behavior problem go on for a few months, even a year or two. When they finally do reach out for help, they're at the end of their rope and want the problem solved immediately." For this reason, having an accessible, reliable community resource at pet owners' fingertips can sometimes make the difference between keeping or surrendering a pet.

Another aid to prospective pet owners worried about behavior issues was a program that began in 1993 to allow adopters to rent training crates directly from OHS for just $5 per month, up to six months.

Human expectations of pet behavior have changed as the animals have increasingly become actual family members, rather than "dumb beasts" kept outside. Accordingly, pet training has evolved as well. Starting in 1965, the OHS Superintendent—then James Zimmer—was named as an official to test obedience-trained dogs for the City of Portland. Under the Police Code, dogs who passed the test could accompany police officers on Portland streets without physical restraints.

One animal whose life was undoubtedly saved thanks to the OHS foster care program was a kitten named Carter. During a routine pre-surgical exam for a neuter surgery, OHS veterinary assistant Shannon Phillips noticed that Carter was breathing heavily, a troubling sign. An X-ray showed that he had a severe condition called pectus excavatum. This meant that Carter's heart had been pushed off to one side, producing a dangerous heart condition. The plan to neuter Carter was put on hold so Dr. Kristi Ellis could fashion a sort of "reverse corset"—a cast around Carter's thorax. The veterinary team then surgically sutured Carter's sternum (breastbone) to his chest so that it would pull away from his spine as he grew. As Phillips recalled, "He was such a little trouper, wearing his weird cast for two months!" But the device was a success. Before long, Carter had his cast removed, got neutered and was adopted by a family with another young kitten. Phillips admitted she had mixed feelings: "It was hard to bring him back after foster." She made a video of Carter learning to walk with his strange new cast: *youtube.com/watch?v=7SJYGxHHmII*.

Humane education also means enlightening pet owners about proper care, what to expect from their animal companions and how to cope with different animal behaviors.

Strangely enough, some prospective owners seem to think that pets will come to them fully versed in the rules of sit, stay and heel. They assume their new friends will be housetrained, and will welcome strangers, walk nicely on a leash and avoid chewing their favorite footwear.

When this does not happen, owners may seek to surrender their pets rather than asking for training in how to help the animals adapt. Through its Behavior and Training team, OHS strives to keep more pets in homes by teaching pet owners positive-reinforcement and responsible methods of animal care. In 2007, OHS opened the Animal Medical Learning Center. Classes ranging from puppy kindergarten to Reactive Rover to Animal Agility are held in Vollum Manners Hall, named to honor the late Jean Vollum's final gift to OHS.

Numerous studies have shown the value of bringing the unconditional love of pets to people in hospitals, hospices, schools and other locales. In 1986, a grant from the Leslie G. Ehmann Trust allowed OHS to hire a part-time coordinator, Jeanne Vernon, to develop its pet therapy program. The Ehmann Trust gift provided funds for Vernon to contact residential care facilities, train and schedule volunteers and document program activities. In 1997, OHS Animal Assisted therapy volunteers and their animals visited more than 15,000 hospital, nursing home and hospice patients. With continuing support from Ehmann Trustees Gordon and Charlotte Childs, in 2007 OHS began offering classes to train people and their pets to pass the certification exam to become licensed Pet Partners. The classes take place in Vollum Manners Hall.

Behavior team volunteers help address shelter dogs' behavior issues.

NEED BEHAVIOR HELP?

Contact OHS's free Behavior Helpline (503-416-2983)

Socializing puppies is an important part of the Behavior Team's efforts.

Agility training with OHS Behavior Team member Jenna Kirby gives dogs like Charlie physical exercise and mental stimulation to keep them healthy and happy.

Best Friends' Corner: Best Little Pet Boutique in Town

16

Can't be sending our newly adopted pets home looking shabby, can we? On May 3, 1986, OHS marked the beginning of Be Kind to Animals Week by opening a spiffy new pet boutique inside the shelter. Best Friends' Corner, so named because it was tucked away in a small space formerly occupied by the old cat haven, was enlarged with the move to the new OHS shelter.

Along with cool accessories such as fluorescent collars and ergonomic pet beds, the new shop adjoining the OHS lobby offers high quality pet foods, grooming accessories, toys and bowls guaranteed to make even the fussiest four-legged eater want to dig in. Inexpensive leashes and collars are available for owners on a tight budget. There's even an array of pet-themed greeting cards and books, and a chic selection of OHS logo-wear. It's not just our opinion that this is one awesome establishment. Readers of *Willamette Week* voted Best Friends' Corner the best pet boutique in Portland in 2003.

Best Friends' Corner in the old shelter.

Today, the OHS boutique is spacious and welcoming.

17

Veterinary Care

With its wide wingspan of services, OHS has always been far more than a mere animal shelter. Caring for creatures has meant an ongoing focus on health and well-being, not just placement. An OHS budget from 1917 notes a salary of $60 per month for a veterinarian—$25 less than the office clerk was paid each month. That year, the vet treated 91 fire horses, 86 street cleaning horses and one Park Bureau horse. Free treatment was also extended to 77 other animals.

Portland pet owners have often turned to OHS, sometimes for rather unusual procedures. Dogs, in particular, are known for their omnivorous tendencies, eating everything from handbags to Big Macs lying on the sidewalk. Often, what goes down needs some help in coming out, and that is where OHS takes over. In 1922, the owners of a feisty little fox terrier brought him in, sheepishly admitting that the dog had been playing with a fish hook that had become lodged in his throat. All it took was patience, a deft hand and a local anesthetic for the OHS technician to remove the offending object.

But Disease has always been a danger for animals living in close confines. By the mid-1960s, OHS Superintendent James Zimmer was recommending that all dogs entering the shelter should be inoculated against distemper. The $1.50 cost for each dog, Zimmer reasoned, could be passed on to the family adopting the animal "Fine, healthy dogs brought to the shelter, if not adopted at once, begin coughing within 10 days and may develop distemper—which means that they must be put to sleep," Zimmer said. But his own board of trustees resisted, arguing that many people did not believe in distemper inoculations, and fearing that if an adopted dog were to become sick and die soon after leaving the shelter, the new owner might blame OHS and bring a lawsuit.

Around the same time, Zimmer convened a meeting with several OHS board members, the OHS general counsel and three representatives of the Portland Veterinary Medical Association (PVMA). The purpose was to discuss cooperation in a program for the betterment of animals in Portland. Several steps were quickly put in place. The first was for the OHS board president to attend monthly PVMA meetings. The next was an agreement that OHS would offer a certificate for a courtesy exam at the vet of an animal adopter's choice. The PVMA also agreed to answer emergency calls when OHS was closed.

Drs. Otteman (left) and Miller (right) with their first cohort of veterinary students.

Even though not all the vets in town were on board with the plan, by June 1964, the PVMA voted to provide the free exams. The veterinarians also agreed to make a list of on-call veterinarians, one or more of whom would be available to serve the public 24 hours a day in cases of emergencies. The plan took full effect in November of that same year. Fifty-one free-exam certificates were provided, and 21 animals were returned to the shelter after doctors found them to be sick with distemper, sore throat or fever.

"Mr. Rutherford had pointed out that after all, veterinarians make their living on animal care—many of the dogs and cats they treat and charge for, originally come from the humane society."

~ OHS Board Minutes, 1966

Two years later, Dr. Gary Bryan of the Willamette Dog and Cat Hospital, president of the Portland Veterinary Medical Association (PVMA), wrote a letter to OHS suggesting that a veterinarian be elected to the OHS Board. The move for increased collaboration between OHS and the PVMA was occurring at precisely the time that national veterinary associations were urging cooperation with local humane societies. The OHS board was struggling with managing the costs of veterinary bills left unpaid by owners of stray and injured animals when they reclaimed their pets, and Dr. Bryan was consulted about the urgency of providing veterinary services for injured dogs. Dr. Bryan advised that a humane society attendant or a veterinarian could administer a tranquilizer—orally, by injection or through a drop on the tongue—that would allow the animal to be sedated for 24-48 hours without further injury. Bryan explained that this would provide time for an injured animal's condition and chances of survival to be evaluated. Bryan also reported that there were always at least two veterinarians on emergency duty, one for Portland's East side, and one for the West.

In 1971, OHS took another bold step by sending every adopted dog or cat home with a month's free pet health insurance. Only a fraction of pet owners continued the insurance but the gesture was seen as a useful tool to encourage responsible pet care. Today, as improvements in veterinary care permit animals to lead longer lives, pet insurance rates remain relatively low. According to *Forbes* magazine, just 2 percent of U. S. pet owners maintained health insurance for their pets.

"In 1971, the OHS Magazine asked 'Is there need for Medical Insurance for Pets? Will the day come when you must decide whether to pay for costly treatment or surgery for a pet? Today, every cat and dog adopted at OHS goes home with a free month's pet health insurance. While only a minority of pet owners carry the insurance, it is recognized as a useful tool to make sure our pets get care they need.'"

~ *OHS Magazine*, 1971

The distemper inoculation controversy had become a non-issue by 1975, when about 100 local veterinarians were donating their time to inoculate incoming animals at OHS. The inoculation program expanded to allow veterinary technician students from Portland Community College to assist in the procedures.

The sophistication of OHS veterinary services continued to move forward. In January 1993 the board voted to hire an animal health technician, replacing an open position for an animal care technician. The move meant OHS could be more effective in blood screening and diagnosing animals available for adoption. At the time, the OHS Executive Committee saw this as "a fairly good substitute for an on-staff veterinarian." The new animal health technician, for instance, would be able to administer a new, integrated vaccine that protected canines against seven diseases.

Still, there were those who wondered why OHS did not have a staff veterinarian. The truth was, no shelter in Oregon had a veterinary clinic as part of its facility, and only the 80 most progressive shelters in the country had veterinarians on site. OHS felt fortunate to have all its veterinary care donated by local veterinarians.

Profile
DR. DON MCCOY:
ALL SHIPS RISE WITH THE TIDE

When Dr. Don McCoy began working with OHS in the early 1970s and became the first vet to serve on the OHS board, he admitted he was a little intimidated by the affluence of so many of his fellow board members. McCoy had just launched his own veterinary practice in North Portland. As a young veterinarian, he knew that many shelter animals were sick with preventable diseases. When the Portland Veterinary Medicine Association (PVMA) asked local vets to volunteer to vaccinate shelter animals, he stepped right up to participate. With a veterinarian on board, OHS could buy and administer rabies vaccines.

So much has changed in the way veterinarians think and practice, McCoy noted. Early on, cats were housed in individual cages, rather than in the communal Moreland Cattery. "We didn't think cats socialized well," he said. He added that the old cattery had poor ventilation. Improved air quality was needed to control infections.

"The changes in vaccination and euthanasia were major," McCoy continued. Using sodium pentobarbital was a more humane way to perform euthanasia than the high altitude chamber located near the OHS barn. McCoy had to "lend" his Drug Enforcement Administration (DEA) certifications so OHS could buy the controlled substance. Some local vets met with resistance when they provided care for the shelter animals in their private practices, since some critics thought that vaccinations and spays and neuters should be limited to private practices. McCoy explained to others in the veterinary community that by helping OHS vets to take care of shelter pets, they were

(Continued on next page)

Dr. Don McCoy & Melinda McCoy enjoy a festive occasion at the OHS shelter.

(Continued from previous page)

freeing up private practices to focus on other treatments. A majority of private-practice vets eventually came around to McCoy's point of view. He called the OHS on-site training program for OSU veterinary students a major step forward in veterinary education.

In fact, the Holman Medical Center at OHS is one of McCoy's proudest achievements. McCoy served on the task force that helped design the clinic, and on the hiring committee interviewing Dr. Kris Otteman, who joined OHS in 2006 as Director of Shelter Medicine. McCoy also heaps praise on the OHS Behavior and Training Team.

But it is Sharon Harmon who earns the bulk of McCoy's admiration. He calls Harmon "the driving force in the organization that raises the bar for animal shelters and humane societies," adding, "She's brought most of the animal rescue groups together, supporting them to reach their goals and help each other. It has been said that all ships rise with the tide."

Even in retirement, Dr. McCoy continues to provide pre-adoption dental care to OHS shelter pets. After OHS confiscated a large number of smaller dogs a few years ago, McCoy offered his help, knowing "small dogs have bad mouths." An early riser, McCoy started walking dogs before his 9 a. m. dental shift and soon joined the OHS Monday morning dog-walking team. McCoy's experience as a climber, caver and scuba diver led him to join the OHS Technical Animal Rescue team in the spring of 2017.

THE OREGON HUMANE SOCIETY
RECOGNIZES THE FOLLOWING
VETERINARIANS
WHO HAVE GENEROUSLY CONTRIBUTED
THEIR TIME AND LEADERSHIP TO
HELP MAKE THIS SHELTER A REALITY

MURRAYHILL VETERINARY HOSPITAL
DONALD E. McCOY, DVM
ROBERT T. FRANKLIN, DVM
GREGG K. TAKASHIMA, DVM
DONALD L. CRIMMINS, DVM
12-MILE ANIMAL CLINIC
ALOHA DOG & CAT HOSPITAL
FRONTIER VETERINARY HOSPITAL
CAROL J. HELFER, DVM
HOLLYWOOD PET HOSPITAL
DR. ROBERT J. ANDERSON
DR. ANNE LAZAR
DR. & MRS. TIMOTHY McCARTHY
MILWAUKIE ANIMAL CLINIC
SUSAN D. MORGAN, VMD
PET SAMARITAN CLINIC
PORTLAND VETERINARY MEDICAL ASSOCIATION
DR. BILL PEMBERTON & DR. DAVID A. BARNO
RALEIGH HILLS VETERINARY HOSPITAL
WILLOWBROOK VETERINARY HOSPITAL
DR. JO-ANNE WISNIEWSKI

RICHARD W. THORESEN, DVM • FREDERICK W. LABAVITCH, DVM •
LINWOOD ANIMAL CLINIC • DR. WENDY WELSH • STEVEN F. SKINNER, DVM •
DR. KEITH D. NICOL • DR. BECKY MARKS & DR. MERLE MARKS •
VETERINARY DIAGNOSTIC IMAGING & CYTOPATHOLOGY • DR. & MRS. STEVEN BATY •
HART ROAD ANIMAL HOSPITAL • DR. ROBERT & NANCY KROLL •
DR. ROBERT MURTAUGH • DR. MARK OYAMA • DR. JEFFREY R. PROULX •
HUGH LEWIS, DVM • MICHAEL G. GADD, DVM • DR. BOB LOBINGIER •
DR. KATHERYN WHITE • VANESSA PRINS WARREN, DVM • DR. COURTNEY WOODSIDE

BETHANY FAMILY PET CLINIC • JULIE DeCAIRE, DVM • LAURA WOOD, DVM • ARGAY CAT CLINIC •
EAGLE FERN VETERINARY HOSPITAL • DR. FRANCESCA GOOD • PAUL HAUGHOM, DVM •
SHERWOOD FAMILY PET CLINIC • DR. SUSAN NOLTE • DR. DANIEL T. O'LOUGHLIN •
DR. MARK E. BURGESS • DR. LAURA B. STROM • JAMES L. WEIKUM, DVM • MICHAEL ZEHENDNER, DVM •
KERRI JACKSON • KENT SMITH, DVM • MEG FREY, DVM • DR. KALI WILSON • DEBRA E. BARNES, DVM •
DR. HEATHER L. HERSHEY • SUSAN E. KIRSCHNER, DVM • DAVID A. ONISHI, DVM •
LES PERRY, DVM • DR. LYNN SHANKS • TOWN & COUNTRY ANIMAL HOSPITAL •
CHERYL I. WARNER, DVM • MONA WILLIAMS, DVM • DR. LISA BERGER • MERRY C. CRIMI, DVM

OHS honors the many Portland-area veterinarians who have donated their skills to help shelter animals.

After years of collaborative planning, OHS teamed up with the College of Veterinary Medicine at Oregon State University (OSU) to open the nation's first in-shelter teaching hospital for veterinary students in 2007. A three-week rotation at OHS's state-of-the-art veterinary medical facility is required for all fourth-year OSU vet students. The aspiring veterinarians hit the ground running at OHS, performing spay-and-neuter procedures, diagnosing diseases and working with prospective pet owners the day they arrive. They work under the close eye of OSU professor Dr. Kirk Miller and the OHS medical team. In addition to educating a new generation of veterinary students, Dr. Miller is advancing veterinary science by exploring the treatment of anorexia in shelter cats, and evaluating the safety and efficiency of high quality/high volume spay/neuter techniques.

"During the first 48 hours, the students generally are hesitant and a bit nervous," said OHS shelter medicine director Dr. Kris Otteman, herself an OSU alumna. "By the middle of the second week, they are competent and confident. By the time they leave, they are old pros."

Teaching began the very day the medical center opened, Sept. 18, 2007, Dr. Otteman recalled. The first four students came in—one of them not so sure she would stay. Instead of the dark, smelly, old facility she had imagined, the student found herself part of a professional medical team in a hospital setting. After she looked around a bit, the student decided to stay. By the end of her two-week rotation, she was asking if she could stay longer.

Profile
KRIS OTTEMAN, D.V.M.

When the shiny new OHS teaching hospital opened in 2007, there was no grand plan for establishing some sort of national model. No one voiced ambitious dreams of transforming veterinary curricula throughout the country to include more than the standard one-hour course on recognizing and responding to animal cruelty. No one could have imagined that care for animals at OHS would improve so dramatically that a euthanasia room would become so superfluous that it was repurposed as the ringworm ward.

And yet, agreed Dr. Kris Otteman, the OHS director of shelter medicine, that is exactly what happened.

"It is so fun to think about," she said during a rare quiet moment in her office. "Even though OHS had been a leader for so long, I think all people really expected was that we weren't going to have to transfer so many animals for spay-and-neuter. I knew we could do so much more."

(Continued on next page)

(Continued from previous page)

In the early days of the hospital, the medical team numbered just six. Now almost 30 people make up the staff. By the end of the first year, 80-90 percent of the Oregon State University veterinary students were asking to stay on beyond their two-week rotations, so the time that students were required to live and work at OHS was expanded to three weeks. While Otteman and her team would be the first to admit that they had been inadvertent trailblazers, a seismic realignment in veterinary education was taking place right before their eyes.

"There was the innovation of having the students here with us, on site," Otteman said. "None of the other veterinary schools had really been able to teach in this hands-on way."

Today, she added, almost every veterinary school in the country has followed suit by establishing some kind of shelter partnership. What a giant change this represents, Otteman said, from the early days when veterinary medicine worldwide focused on protecting humans and providing food and transportation.

Students at OHS began working with shelter animals the minute they walk through the door, learning on the job the skills that would translate not only to confidence, competence and compassion, but also to increased employability. Every day brought new, unpredictable challenges—exactly what the students could expect to encounter as they graduated and entered veterinary practice of their own. Otteman remembered one dog, a setter named Gordie, who had been released for euthanasia by the time she and her students got to see him. Gordie had been in a terrible car accident, with severe wounds to three of his limbs.

"We bandaged that dog for six weeks, and he healed and went on to a happy new home," Otteman said.

That kind of willingness to take a risk on an animal that might otherwise have been written off characterizes a certain spirit that is part of the fabric of OHS, Otteman believes.

"OHS for years has been willing to step out there and try things," she said. "There's a lot of support here for trying new things, just seeing if they will work. There's a 'yes' culture here, a readiness to 'just say yes' whenever you can. The benefit to people and animals here is huge."

That atmosphere of encouragement makes OHS and Otteman a perfect match.

"I'm always thinking about what to do newer, smarter, faster, cheaper," she said. "I'm a developer, a startup person. Sitting still is not very comfortable for me."

But when it comes to establishing and maintaining a stable, supportive environment, Otteman also was quick to extend credit to the steady presence of the OHS leadership team. OHS maintains a sense of vision, she continued. And she hailed the nexus at OHS between academics, veterinary care and a concern for animal welfare.

As OHS looks to the future—its New Road Ahead—Otteman cited a strategic vision that will center on continuing leadership in the industry, the best possible care for the pets and "a dedicated belief that we have to keep educating."

One of Otteman's own first lessons was that it was a whole lot easier to spay or neuter an animal than to try to explain to a veterinary student how to perform the same task. But the first such procedure went smoothly, and Otteman exhaled. Things were going to be just fine.

The model of partnering with an animal shelter was so novel, and so intriguing, that delegates from 100 percent of the veterinary schools in the U. S. showed up at an OHS conference on innovation in 2008. Ten years later, almost every U.S. veterinary school has some sort of shelter partnership.

At OHS, the students live above the hospital, in spiffy dorm rooms that make their commute to work a brisk two minutes. It was common for students to request to stay on beyond their required two weeks, and so in 2013, the rotation expanded to three weeks. The work is that stimulating, and that germane to what they will be doing as professional veterinarians.

With three surgical suites, a digital X-ray unit, a laboratory, pharmacy and comfortable recovery rooms for cats and dogs, the Thomas W. and Mary D. Holman Medical Center has fast become a national model. More than 12,000 surgeries are performed there annually, starting with making sure that every cat, dog and rabbit adopted from OHS has been spayed or neutered. Thousands of other pets are neutered at little or no cost as part of a "Spay and Save" program serving low-income families. Coupled with its aggressive spay and neuter campaign, the high level of care and attention provided at the Holman Medical Center is a major part of why OHS has maintained a near-zero euthanasia rate.

The high level of care and attention provided at the center is a major part of why OHS has maintained a near-zero euthanasia rate.

The medical center also provides veterinary expertise to support humane investigations and crucial experience for the next generation of Oregon veterinarians. "We put them to work," said Otteman. "This is exactly the kind of experience that will make students into better professionals—learning about high volume, high quality medicine and surgery in a state-of-the-art facility."

The idea for the collaboration between OHS and the OSU veterinary school can be credited to OHS staff and board leadership, but the impetus for this sparkling and innovative medical center came from a $1 million estate gift from prominent Portland resident, Thomas W. Holman Sr. A fourth-generation Portland resident on both sides of his family, Holman grew up playing with cats and dogs on his family's farm in Estacada. He and Mary Dooly married in 1947. Holman worked for 42 years with the traffic division of Union Pacific Railroad. Holman was present and smiling with pride as the ribbon was cut on the new OHS medical center named for him and his late wife. He died in 2013, just shy of his 100th birthday.

To showcase outstanding examples of shelters in action, Maddie's Fund—a national animal welfare philanthropy—installed a camera in 2015 so that anyone can watch procedures underway in the Coit Family Surgery Suite at OHS. Take a peek:

maddiesfund.org/maddiecam-oregon-humane-society. htm

Honoring Thomas Holman at the groundbreaking of the medical center named for him and his late wife with kisses from OHS staffers Marsha Chrest and Nicole Edson.

Three generations of the Coit family visiting the surgery named for their generosity.

19

Outreach

Community outreach extends beyond the partnerships OHS has forged with the Portland Veterinary Medical Association and with the OSU College of Veterinary Medicine. When OHS teemed with an overabundance of animals, OHS personnel were willing to transport the pets far and wide to help them find loving homes. This often meant working with reputable pet supply stores, who saw the OHS animals as a major customer draw, or with businesses, sports programs and houses of worship.

In 1993, OHS had reached a save rate of about 80 percent for dogs. That still left a significant number in need of homes. That year, Petco began providing space where OHS volunteers could process adoptions. The next year, a new PetSmart store in Tigard offered a permanent "Luv a Pet" space for OHS adoptions. In 1995 alone, 370 dogs, cats, rabbits, rats, hamsters and gerbils found homes through the OHS-PetSmart partnership.

Adoptions also took place at Portland Rockies baseball games, at Trail Blazers basketball games and at the Portland headquarters of the advertising agency Wieden+Kennedy. A deaf, older Sheltie was among the pets placed at Pet Loft, courtesy of manager Bill LaPolla. Lucky Lab Brewery organized "adoptions on tap," and rabbits found new guardians through Rabbit Advocates. Foster dogs even visited local churches in search of friendly parishioners to offer them forever homes.

Today, however, the supply and demand equation has rebalanced. The number of local animals available for adoption has dwindled dramatically, thanks to targeted spay and neuter efforts. Meantime, the flow of visitors to OHS grows steadily, with at least 130,000 people passing through the doors annually. Outreach programs, however, continue to inform the public of services offered by OHS and to help raise funds.

OHS staff and volunteers take part in many city parades and festivals.

It is not uncommon to see area residents arriving at OHS with armloads of handmade gifts for the animals. The holiday season brings the giving tree, festooned with photos of OHS shelter animals. Visitors leave food, toys and other presents under the big tree in the lobby. Starting each Dec. 1, the lobby also is adorned with photos of all the pets in the shelter on that date. OHS makes a commitment to send each one of them "home for the holidays" before the end of the year.

Move Over, Hollywood

Who needs "Best in Show"? On Sept. 10, 1936, Mrs. C. S. Jackson launched what was to become a city tradition. The "All American

Mutt Show" actually began as a birthday party for her grandson Peter Jackson Jr., held in the upstairs room at OHS. Each of Peter's friends was invited to bring his or her dog to the party. While the children ate cake and ice cream, Mrs. Jackson served bones to the dogs. The celebrations continued annually, even as Peter Jackson grew up and had a son of his own. Beyond bones, Mrs. Jackson handed out licenses, dog food and vouchers for free inoculations. Soon enough, the tradition became the All-American Mutt show, where mixed breeds—sometimes known as Kenardlys, because you "can 'ardly" tell where they came from—came from near and far for their day of glory.

Presiding as judges at the 1942 Mutt Show were, left to right, Kenneth Cooper, City Commissioner; Earl Snell, Secretary of State; C. F. Wiegand, Park Bureau; Lew Wallace, State Senator; Harvey Wells, State Representative; Harry Daniel, President of OHS, and their canine friends.

In 1942, Larry McClung of the *Oregon Journal* began promoting the Mutt Show through his newspaper. McClung recalled in 1985 how one year, six little Sellwood neighborhood kids pooled their pennies so their pups could take part in the Mutt Show. They called a cab, whose driver unceremoniously dumped the kids and their dogs at OHS and told them not to call him back. Humane society staffers happily drove them back home.

By 1964, *The Oregonian* was sponsoring the Mutt Show. Two years later, Quaker Oats and Meier & Frank joined in the sponsorship. The thirty-fifth Mutt Show, held Sept. 12, 1970, was jointly sponsored by *The Oregonian* and OHS.

As she handed out dog bones and cake and ice cream at that first event in 1936, Mrs. Jackson would have been hard pressed to imagine the dimensions the Mutt Show would take on. In 1984, nearly 2,000 spectators gathered at the Lloyd Center to cheer for 150 local dogs.

At the 57th Annual Mutt Show and Pedigree "Pet" Athlon, held on Sept 12, 1992, Olympic gymnast Peter Vidmar emceed the affair, which brought in more than $14,000 for OHS. In 1985, the event featured Bill Schonely, the voice of the Portland Trail Blazers, as emcee, and *Oregonian* columnist Jonathan Nicholas as one of the judges. The ceremonies began with a display of what was believed to be the largest dog biscuit ever made, created by Blue Mountain Pet Foods for the Mutt Show's fiftieth anniversary. Mayor Bud Clark signed a proclamation declaring Sept. 14, 1985, as "All American Mutt Day" in the City of Roses. "We have been endowed with the blessings and benefits of our mixed-breed canine friends, who give us companionship and great pleasure in our lives," the mayor intoned. Mutt of the Year award went to Patrick Ryan's dog Sparky.

Among the Mutt Show's early features was a four-legged race to see who was the fastest mutt. In 1985, this part of the fun morphed into a Dog Walk-a-Thon, and in 1988, the OHS Doggie Dash began. By 2017, the Dash had become the largest OHS fund raising event, generating $680,000 and bringing about 8,000 people (and 3,500 dogs) to downtown Portland. The city's Naito Parkway is closed off for the occasion, and dogs are allowed on Tri-Met for this one particular day. It is the largest charity dog walk in the West.

Thousands of dog lovers crowd Naito Parkway at the start of the 2017 Doggie Dash.

Holidays also bring public events to benefit OHS. In 1986, 2,400 Easter eggs were found in record time at the annual hunt, now a thing of the past. The speedy scavenging prompted the board to suggest doubling the number of hidden eggs to 400 dozen for the next hunt.

And Santa Paws! Who doesn't want a picture of their pet with the jolly old gent? With sponsorship from Fred Meyer, Whiskas, Pedigree and others, the annual opportunity to nab a photo of Felix the cat or Joey the Jack Russell sitting on Santa's lap has become a holiday tradition for many Portland families.

Naughty or nice? The jolly old gentleman checks in with Portland pets.

Animals are important to many faith traditions. In 1998, Tom and Susan Stern created, sponsored and hosted Mitzpaw Day, a special celebration at the Mittleman Jewish Community Center to benefit the campaign to build a new shelter. As Susan Stern explained, "The Torah teaches us to have compassion for animals because as humans we have the responsibility of being charged with caring for creation, and leaving it better than we found it. The way we treat animals defines us as individuals and as a culture. Our ability to be kind and compassionate toward animals is directly linked with our ability to have compassion for people."

"The way we treat animals defines us as individuals and as a culture."

~ Susan Stern

As a beloved institution in Portland, OHS has participated in many community-based events that help generate public support and also provide good publicity. OHS trustees, for example, have helped sell tickets to the annual Street of Dreams project. Prizes at the "Fore-Footed Friends" golf tournament included the "Benji Hogan Buried Bone" prize for the biggest divot and "Rover's All Over" award for the golfer spending the most time in the rough. The Pedigree Pentathlon, a sort of Doggie Olympics, started in 1990. Winning snapshots submitted to the yearly Fuzzy, Furry and Feathered Friends Photo contest adorn the walls at OHS.

OHS also received some plugs in the form of billboards featuring Bob the Weather Cat. Bob, whose actual name was Hank, was a kind of kitty clothes horse who had become a sensation on KATU-TV.

Which way is the wind blowing? Only Bob the Weathercat knew for sure.

In 2000, OHS partnered with PetSmart to promote a telethon designed to showcase adoptions and raise awareness about animal issues. Emceed for many years by KINK-FM radio host Les Sarnoff, the telethon also produced significant support. The 2016 telethon broke fundraising records when it brought in $495,184 in donations.

20

Galas and Fundraisers

If you're going to ask people to pony up for a new shelter, you'd better do it with music and a lot of flowing bubbly. "Gimme Shelter" rocked the staid Heathman Hotel in 1998. Turns out pet lovers also like to cut up the dance floor. That night, music was provided by Five Guys Named Moe.

Revelers raise their bid cards high at the 2014 Fetch gala.

Mid-20th Century revelers at an OHS gala.

In 2007, FETCH the Ball honored Ernest Swigert and Dolorosa Margulis, to whom the current shelter is dedicated, in gratitude for their leadership of the campaign to build it, and Thomas W. Holman, after whom the new Thomas W. and Mary D. Holman Medical Center is named. Even though it was held on an exceedingly hot day in July 2013, FETCH Silver brought out more than 300 people determined to honor Executive Director Sharon Harmon for her 25 years of remarkable service, no matter what the weather. Just to make sure Harmon knew how much she was appreciated, Ellyn Bye pledged $25,000—and then another $10,000!—to encourage Harmon to remain on the job for another ten years.

Profile

DOLOROSA MARGULIS

"Save the animals: It's the best gift you can give," said Dolorosa Margulis, past Board Chair and one of the first four recipients of the OHS Lifetime Achievement Diamond Collar Award, along with Ernie Swigert, Les Sarnoff and Howard Hedinger.

On the lookout in the mid-1980s for new OHS board members, Dolorosa Margulis made the acquaintance of Portland businessman and philanthropist Ernest C. Swigert. Margulis promptly recruited Swigert, and forged a rare partnership that succeeded in enhancing both the public image and the buildings of OHS.

"I miss Ernie every day," Margulis said of her friend who passed away in 2008. "He was such a sweetheart and a real character. Life seems empty without him."

It didn't hurt that Swigert spoke fluent Dutch, Margulis' native language, and also knew her parents. Their partnership in support of OHS flourished.

"We were co-conspirators," she said, "working on behalf of OHS."

A born animal lover, Margulis has always had both cats and dogs. In her home country of The Netherlands, pets were viewed as extensions of the family. The example of kindness toward animals came from the top, right from the royal family of The Netherlands. Queen Juliana, Margulis remembered, "was a nice lady who loved animals."

Dolorosa adopted a six-week-old puppy from OHS and had him for 14 years. She went on to adopt a large, mature cat, and later, two Borzois, or Russian wolfhounds, as well as a Bouvier. Nearly all her animals came from OHS. Margulis was one of the first people to adopt an animal enrolled in the Friends Forever program. The white cat had outlived its owner, and even though the grumpy feline bit Dolorosa, she adopted the cat to keep her farm manager company.

"Animals are not a commodity," she believes. "They're very important and they're sentient beings."

Like so many others who worked or volunteered at the old OHS shelter, Margulis called it a dismal place. The place was drafty and leaks abounded. Margulis set about using her extensive social connections in Portland to seek donations to build a new shelter for OHS. Her specialty was brunch: a lovely meal followed by a pitch for funds for OHS. Donations poured in.

Dolorosa and Swigert lived across the street from one another. Swigert, in particular, loved to host parties with good food and wine. Their guests were willing participants in their plot to weaken their wallets. "Our strategy was to connect with people who loved animals and ask them for money to help," she explained.

Margulis has another partner-in-crime in the form of her husband, David, proprietor of Margulis Jewelers. One of the family dogs would often accompany David Margulis to the store in downtown Portland. When a client would pet the dog or strike up a doggie-human conversation, David took every opportunity to extol the virtues of the Oregon Humane Society.

Looking back on her long, happy affiliation with OHS, Margulis said some programs stand out: animal population control through neuter and spay program, education on the humane treatment of animals, and improved space for shelter animals while they await adoption.

She remains a fierce advocate for tough laws to protect animals. "We have to be vigilant and protect animals, so laws are very important, to apply and enforce the laws we have in place," she says.

When OHS Executive Director Dale Dunning stepped down in 1998, Margulis urged that Sharon Harmon be selected to replace him. Margulis had worked with Harmon as operations director for eight years and felt strongly that Harmon had proved herself up to the job. But others on the board wanted to hire a headhunter to conduct a national search to find a new executive director. Margulis remained staunch in her support, and when the nationwide search led to Margulis' own first choice for the job, Sharon Harmon, Margulis was thrilled. Since then, she said, "she has exceeded my expectations as OHS executive director. Sharon is a confident, progressive leader who demonstrates imagination and is respectful of staff. She grew into the leader she is today."

When enough money was raised to build a new shelter and the sparkling new facility was dedicated in 2000, Sen. Mark Hatfield turned to Margulis and asked her to cut the ribbon. Her leadership, and Swigert's, are honored in a plaque at the main entrance to the shelter they were determined would be built.

"It was a lot of fun and gratifying to see the shelter become reality," she said.

Today, Margulis serves as honorary chair of the New Road Ahead initiative, seeking always to advance the well-being of her beloved animals and the institution that serves them.

OHS, she says, "is a place of life and joy."

Dolorosa and David Margulis flank Ernest Swigert at the 1991 OHS poster judging.

Seizing on the popular vernacular of the day, in 2002, OHS chose the cuddly phrase "Feel the Love" to go with a redesigned logo, designed by Sandstrom Partners.

 OREGON
HUMANE
SOCIETY

"End Petlessness" came along in 2007.

In 1985, OHS decided to be known as the "Be Kind to Animals" people.

An ancient formula of American newspapers still holds true: Put a picture of a kid or a pet on the front page and your sales that day will skyrocket. Make it a picture of a kid and a pet and the newsstands will sell out. So it is with television and radio as well. Universally, the public loves a feel-good story about animals. Emotions about animals run strong: Public outrage explodes over any story about animal cruelty.

Still, it wasn't until the mid-20th century that OHS formally recognized the need, as one board report from 1943 put it, to keep "happy relations" with the press. The same year brought an understanding of how important it was for OHS to be transparent about its operations. In order to maintain public confidence and the trust of the city and state government, there should be no "air of mystery" about OHS, the board agreed.

Starting around 1956, KOIN-TV host Doris Kyber gave OHS a boost when she began featuring OHS animals on her show *Hi Neighbor*. This popular element of the show continued through the mid-1960s. When the *Sally Sunday* show made its debut on KGW-TV in 1967, Warren Cox, the new OHS executive director, was among the guests. By 1982, OHS was airing its own radio show, *Animal Focus*, on the first Wednesday of each month on KPBS.

Launching a joint spay/neuter campaign in 1991 with the Willamette Humane Society, OHS received national attention for the billboards produced by the Hallock Agency. The message these billboards carried was both disturbing and dramatic.

This 1991 spay/neuter campaign carried a heart-wrenching message.

Way back in November 1922, OHS stepped into the publishing business itself with the launch of *Every Living Creature: Official Organ Oregon Humane Society*. The monthly newsletter billed itself as "a Pacific Coast publication, devoted to the cause of child welfare, animal protection and humane education." Advertising revenue came from such sources as Butler Pullet Farm ("This is a real Honest-to-Goodness Egg Farm") and Rose City Veterinary Hospital.

The first edition of *Every Living Creature* featured horses and a cow
as well as companion animals and a beaver, our state's mascot.

Just under 50 years later, another newsletter called *Your Animals'
Friend* appeared with the goal of showcasing OHS accomplishments
and bringing attention to OHS services. In the 1980s the Society's
publication was renamed *The Oregon Humane Society Speaks*. In 1990,
the publication became *Animal Focus*. Today's printed quarterly, the
Oregon Humane Society Magazine, goes to 30,000 homes, businesses,
organizations and veterinary offices.

OHS publications have changed names through the decades,
but have always celebrated the special place animals have in our lives.

OHS was an early adopter of the move to online publishing. In 1995,
OHS sent the cyber-message: "Browse the internet to find a pet? Yes,
you can!" OHS staffers quickly recognized the value of this new tool,
and pressed for OHS to become one of the country's first humane
societies to launch a website. That initial website, hosted through
teleport.com, featured a daily inventory of dogs. Cats followed

Today, the *Oregon Humane Society Magazine* keeps readers informed about our latest work.

shortly. The site also included an events calendar, business hours, a map giving directions to the shelter and a seven-day listing of stray animals received. Results were immediate. Only a few days after OHS went online, a family arrived at the shelter with the dog inventory printout and their new dog selected. After a get-acquainted visit, the dog went home with his forever family.

In time the website grew more sophisticated, with increased photographic content, and in 1999, its own domain, *oregonhumane.com*. The site soon became a display space for winning posters and essays from the Humane Education contest, winning photos from the Fuzzy, Furry and Feathered Friends photo contest, and photos of construction of the new shelter. In 2001, the web address changed to the site that remains in use today: *oregonhumane.org*.

Today, the OHS website is an indispensable and popular tool, with more than 3 million visits annually to view pets, get information, or donate online. More than $1.4 million was contributed in 2016 through the website from an average of more than 7,100 visitors per day. The OHS Facebook page attracts more than 100,000 followers, and in 2016, OHS had almost 17,000 followers on Instagram, a 110 percent increase over the previous year.

But all the good-news stories and flashy billboards could not always move public perceptions. In 1964, William Rutherford worried that many people continued to think of OHS as a place for animal executions, not a refuge for animals waiting to be adopted into new homes. The OHS board took action with newspaper ads informing readers that "If you want a dog, the Oregon Humane Society has one to please you."

That same year, OHS officials decided to revive a dormant public relations committee. A year later, the board went one step further by hiring Frances Blakely as the new director of public relations. After just three months on the job, Mrs. Blakely asked to work on a volunteer basis.

Today the staff of Community Outreach and Public Information Services produces press releases, events, community and corporate partnerships, the *OHS Magazine* and online services.

OHS merchandise, ready for holiday shoppers.

OHS launched a new ad campaign in 2017 asking people to *#bemorehumane*. Leopold Ketel and Partners created this award winning work.

OHS receives not one dime in government funding, relying only on its loyal and ever-increasing membership base. OHS membership is open to anyone who loves animals and contributes modest dues. The more than 20,000 supporters of OHS come from all Portland neighborhoods, every Oregon county, most U.S. states and many foreign countries. OHS members also reflect different walks of life, economic backgrounds, political ideologies, religions and beliefs. What they share is a powerful commitment to saving and improving the lives of animals. Even in the old days, when OHS served as city poundmaster and received a portion of city dog license fees, the generosity of members was vital to the organization's success.

"The executive committee discussed society finances and lack of sufficient income. It was agreed that the society was gradually going into the red. Mr. Platt suggested that the president appoint a membership committee to plan and execute a campaign for new members—dues-paying members—to supplement society income."

~ OHS Board Minutes, September 17, 1968

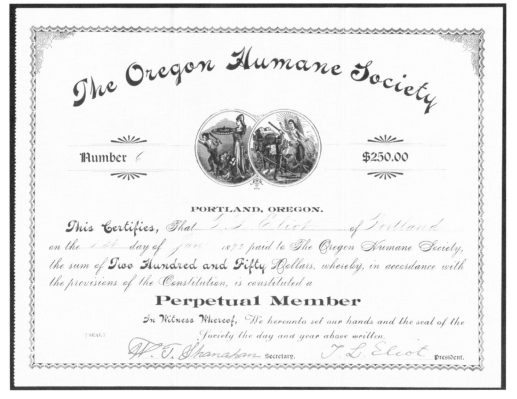

This 1893 perpetual membership certificate guaranteed that founder Thomas Lamb Eliot would remain part of the Oregon Humane Society to this very day.

"For many of the older humane groups I've always thought that it was great to look at the early supporters, board members, donors. The names you find will often be familiar—they are the same names you see on streets, buildings, parks, and other areas of the community. This demonstrates that caring for animals is not just a 'nice' addition to the community. The founders and early leaders of the community felt that it was so important to the culture and welfare of the community that they lent their support, and often money, to ensure that the humane treatment of animals was a core value of the community."

~ Stephen Zawistowski, Ph.D., ASPCA Science Advisor Emeritus

Profile
PHYLLIS AND GERALD PETERSEN
Memories of Beloved Pets Live On for Longtime Members

Phyllis and Gerald Petersen, seen here at the 2004 OHS Tail Wag with Executive Director Sharon Harmon and OHS Trustee Marveita Redding, have been loyal OHS supporters since 1959.

In 1956, Jerry and Phyllis Petersen were about to buy a new Thunderbird. They were discussing which color to buy when they spotted a newspaper ad for boxer dogs. The moment they met the boxer pup Cliffie, it was love at first sight. They quickly nixed the idea of buying a sports car because it wouldn't provide adequate space for a full-grown boxer. After several happy years with Cliffie, they were devastated when he died. Bereft, they wanted to honor Cliffie properly. Their vet advised the Petersens to check out the animal cemetery at Oregon Humane Society. "We did and that was our introduction to OHS," said Phyllis.

The Petersens became OHS members in 1959, and have remained so ever since, an extraordinary run of almost 60 years of loyal support. Charter members of the Thomas Lamb Eliot Circle, they often make the drive from their home in Corvallis to enjoy special events at OHS with the friends they've made over the years. Through the decades the Petersens have shared their life with nine dogs, all now buried in the OHS cemetery. Their last dogs were a female miniature Schnauzer named Abby, along with the dog's older sister, Katy. "Katy had impeccable manners, and we felt she would be a good role model for Abby, and she actually house-trained Abby," Phyllis said. Each year at Christmas, Phyllis and Jerry come to OHS laden with holiday treats for pets at the shelter, and stop to decorate the graves of their dogs Cliffie, Mackie, Dannie, Montie, Herbie, Mandy, Molly, Abbie and Katy.

The Petersens are canine empty-nesters now. They are grateful for the many happy memories they have of their nine precious dogs. "We have a special place in our hearts for OHS, and frequently visit the graves of our beloved dogs," said Phyllis.

Jerry Petersen served on the Oregon Animal Health Foundation where he first met Sharon Harmon. Her vision and drive inspired them to be part of the campaign for the new shelter. They were so pleased when the new facility was built, especially knowing that "not one dime was owed on it." They're proud of the new clinic, too.

"We are most appreciative of OHS, for what it does for the animals, and for what it has done for us personally," said Phyllis. OHS in turn is grateful for the Petersens, whom have helped make OHS what it is today.

An annual OHS membership cost all of $1 in 1922. Life membership came in at $25, and for $250, a donor could become a perpetual member. Life members that year included:

Mary F. and Henrietta Failing, the East & West Lumber Co., Eastside Mill & Lumber Co., the Unitarian Church School, Henry F. Cabell, August Berg, Balfour Gutherie Co., the Ames Harris Neville Co., Allen & Lewis Co. and Mrs. W. B. Ayer.

Other life members were: Edward E. Graff, Mrs. F. F. Griswold, Franklin T. Griffith, Lydis A. Irons, Maria C. Jackson, E. J. Jaeger, Otto Kraemer, Alma D. Katz, S. E. Kraemer, Gay Lombard, Ladd Estate, Ladd & Tilton Bank, Julius L. Meier, Caroline S. Mayes, Meier & Frank Co. and *The Oregonian*. Pacific Export Lumber Co. also claimed life membership, as did Porter Bros., Portland Cordage, Security Savings & Trust Co., Mrs. F. W. Swanton, Genevieve Thompson, Mrs. J. N. Teal, Mrs. D. P. Thompson, Warren Construction Co. and the Weinhard Estate. OHS also counted 362 annual members that year.

With this jaunty patch, OHS members wore their pride on their sleeve.

In 1991, a "Little Bit" fall mailer, styled as a personalized letter from a fictional shelter dog, prompted a membership surge. An ad series in *The Oregonian* that year also brought new members. 30

Some donors defied conventional categories, so OHS made up new descriptions to honor their generosity. In 1965, Mrs. Nita Busterholtz was recognized as "probably the most consistent contributor of cash to the society over the years that the board could remember." A year earlier, the OHS board took note of the potential cache of donations that might be available through estate planning and prepared a letter to remind members of the Oregon Bar Association that their clients might want to consider including OHS in their estate plans. This effort produced quick results. In 1966, Mollie Mignon Fisher, head of the Multnomah County Library Association research department, left her estate to be divided equally between OHS and the Animal Defenders League—but only after her cat Waffles had been provided with a good home for life. The "Friends Forever" estate-giving plan was stepped up in 2000 with an *OHS Magazine* ad that explained, "In Oregon, you cannot leave money to animals. However, you can make provisions in your will for the care and adoption of your surviving pets…. As a Friends Forever member, you make a significant planned gift to the Oregon Humane Society to help sustain its operation and OHS promises to care for and find new homes for your surviving pets."

Like most nonprofits, OHS has tried many fund-raising paths. In 1974, OHS received $1 from every foil wrapper of a Sergeant's Flea Collar sent in. In 1978, OHS earned $2 from weight seals of certain Purina dog and puppy food sacks. A direct-mail campaign began in 1985, sending appeal letters three times a year. Autos for Animals began in 1983, with a campaign that read "Your old Rabbits, Foxes, Cougars and Eagles can help cats and dogs."

Profile

TOWARD LONG-TERM FINANCIAL STABILITY: GARY KISH

When he started working at OHS late in 1990, Vice President for Development Gary Kish saw the old facility located in an industrial area on Columbia Boulevard as "an oasis of green." But if the shelter looked welcoming from the outside, it was far less appealing inside. The shelter was noisy and crowded, with dogs easily becoming agitated as they faced each other in kennels. Once the barking started, it was pure cacophony. Still, with only a handful of volunteers and a 20-person staff, they managed to find new homes for about 6,000 animals annually.

Kish brought business experience to OHS, and had volunteered with several conservation-oriented non-profits. OHS was a wide-open frontier for fundraising when he signed on. While his original task was to write grant proposals, he quickly introduced new fundraising streams. He hired Tom Jenike to write software programs to implement the monthly donor program, and over the years added staff to provide more technical assistance. He's grown the development program at OHS to include a staff of 14, along with a small army of volunteers.

Kish's main goal was to establish long-term financial stability by creating a diversified funding base. The resulting healthy financial status has shown a 10 percent average growth each year. The only low point he remembers came in the 1990s, was when momentum stalled midway through the first capital campaign to raise money for the new building. He said Sharon Harmon energized the campaign when she became executive director—and eventually, Kish's wife. "Sharon Harmon demonstrated confidence, competence and built trust," he said, "all while inspiring enthusiasm and we finished the campaign strongly."

Under Kish's direction, the PAWS (planned monthly withdrawal program) surpassed the goal of 2,000 participants. His initial goal of building OHS membership to 20,000 has been surpassed, with a 2017 total of about 24,000 supporters. After a long-term supporter contacted Kish to ask about providing care for pets who might outlive her, he launched Friends Forever™. Under this program, donors who include OHS in their wills or other estate plans are guaranteed that OHS will receive, care for and place their pets should the need arise. Kish even worked with attorney J. Alan Jensen to draft language that could be included in a donor's will. In 1999, Gary was a moving force when OHS went to the Oregon legislature to exempt pets from probate and enable legal transfer of ownership. Since 2001, pet trusts in Oregon have been recognized as valid and enforceable. To date, about 1,000 people have included OHS in their estate plans. In winter 1994, Kish worked successfully to secure final approval from the Oregon Insurance Division to offer charitable gift annuities. These annuities support the Society's work and provide donors with guaranteed, fixed-rate, partially tax-free income for life.

Kish had his doubts at first about the "Autos for Animals" program, and was happily surprised when it generated about 1,000 vehicles a year donated to OHS—and then converted to cash. Unlike many other nonprofits, OHS minimizes expenses (and maximizes revenue) by managing its auto donation program internally.

"Successful OHS programs drive fundraising success—we are simply storytellers," said Gary.

But it's the future that has Kish the most excited. "I can't wait to see where OHS ends up ten, twenty or thirty years from now," he said. "We're currently a leading animal organization nationally and internationally which gives us a pretty secure place going forward. I'm confident in the future."

Meanwhile, back on the home front, Kish said being married to the boss has been a happy balancing act. He and Sharon Harmon he said, "have overlapping interests in animal welfare and technical aspects like veterinary medicine. My expertise in fundraising, science and law meshes well with Sharon's expertise in animal welfare, science and zoology. Sharon has the ability to inspire others by being a great leader."

As electronic giving became more feasible, OHS offered donors the option to make automatic monthly donations through a new Planned Account Withdrawal System (PAWS) started in 1995. Today, almost 2,500 families donate monthly to OHS through PAWS, using their checking accounts or credit cards. "Charitable Check-off" began in late 2001, with OHS supporters and volunteers gathering more than 10,000 signatures of Oregon voters to be added to the list of charities on the Oregon tax form to which state residents could dedicate tax refund monies.

But sometimes, the kind of work OHS does has presented certain charitable-giving obstacles. Development Director Gary Kish had to present a forceful argument that OHS directly affects "human health and welfare" in order for OHS to be accepted into the Combined Federal Campaign in 1992. This marked the first time that OHS had participated in a workplace giving/payroll deduction campaign. Notes from that year stressed that the United Way's focus on human health made participation difficult. Still, perseverance paid off. The 1998 campaigns brought in more than $10,000. By fall 1999, OHS was in state and federal workplace giving campaigns, as well as the giving programs of the City of Portland, Metro, Port of Portland, Intel, and Wells Fargo Bank.

OHS has long been mindful of the need to protect its donors' privacy. As early as 1998, OHS issued a statement concerning its "longstanding policy of not selling, trading or otherwise making available the names of its supporters."

Profile

HARVEY BLACK
Influential OHS Board member

Harvey Black worked as a lawyer in San Francisco for 30 years before returning to his native Portland. He and his wife Nancy volunteered to exercise dogs at the old OHS facility. The place was noisy and chaotic, with dogs housed in kennels facing each other. Big dogs easily escaped, and despite calls of "Loose dog," once the kennels were open, dogs sometimes ran into traffic on busy Northeast Columbia Boulevard.

When the position of OHS executive director came open, it was Nancy Black who suggested that Sharon Harmon, already the OHS chief of operations, could do the job. In the mid-1990s, Harvey began attending OHS board meetings and soon applied to join. Today he is one of the longest tenured board members.

No one on the board had much fundraising experience when Harmon set a goal of $6-$8 million for a capital campaign to raise money for the new shelter. They collectively decided to raise the money needed before construction began.

Harvey gave Harmon his enthusiastic backing when she proposed to the board that OHS form a partnership with OSU's veterinary program. Black chaired the capital campaign to raise funds for the medical unit. "OHS was on the cutting edge and set up a unique teaching partnership with the university," Black declared.

Black can't lavish enough praise on Sharon Harmon. Under her leadership, he said, "OHS runs like a Swiss watch."

Major Gifts

It is a truism in nonprofit fundraising that major donors create a dramatic impact on the health and well-being of an organization. In 2004, OHS invested in a new position to create a special program for top donors and hired Mary Henry as the organization's first donor relations manager. Charged with designing an identity for the program, Henry found inspiration in the compassion, dedication and pioneering spirit of founder Thomas Lamb Eliot. The new Thomas Lamb Eliot Circle, or TLC for short, began with 159 members giving $1,000 or more annually. Benefits include invitations to TLC events and the opportunity for a behind-the-scenes tour. In the years since, the TLC circle has grown to almost 1,000 members who provide more than $2 million annually.

Charter TLC members Ellyn Bye and Gordon & Charlotte Childs join Mary Henry at the 2007 celebration of the opening of the Animal Medical Learning Center.

For all its work in finding suitable forever homes for animals, OHS also wanted to make sure the dogs, cats and other creatures had first-class accommodations during their stays at OHS.

Soon after he took office as OHS director in 1967, Warren Cox had cages removed from the receiving room. He had the room painted, and installed a cheerful humane officer at the receiving desk. These small but important changes meant that people giving up their cats and dogs no longer needed to see them locked in grim cages or left in a cold room while they attended to OHS paperwork. Sensitivity about this process grew, and in 2001, OHS began offering pre-admission counseling.

"There is no time limit on dogs and cats in our program for adoption."

Even in 1912, when OHS opened its first area where animals housed in kennels could be adopted, OHS officials recognized that the act of taking home an abandoned dog or cat is fraught with complexities. No one answer explains what motivates a prospective owner to choose one pet over another. But for many years, a higher proportion of dogs than cats found homes. In the winter of 1913-14, for instance, OHS found homes for 63 percent of the dogs that came in, but only 36 percent of the cats.

At one point, in 1944, there was talk of holding special Sunday auctions so dogs could be placed with the highest bidder. But the board decided against this idea, reasoning that the sooner an animal could be placed in a good home, the better. Several years later, OHS officials began to think about keeping better track of animals who left the shelter. If a prospective owner came in soon after he or she had already taken home an OHS animal, officials were instructed to find out why the owner wanted another.

Adoption fees remained low: $4 for male dogs in 1964, of which $3 went to the city license. That year the price for unspayed females was raised, with the hope of reducing the dog population. A Christmas giveaway each year turned into a kind of adoption madhouse, and at least one board member worried that adopters were not adequately screened in the tumult. As a smoother system settled in, OHS was placing more than 600 animals each month into homes in 1970, a much lower adoption rate than in the early years.

More than 70,000 animals were surrendered by their owners to OHS in 1970.

The vexing issue of how to manage the unrelenting onslaught of unwanted animals and how long to keep an animal in the shelter persisted. More than 70,000 animals were surrendered by their owners to OHS in 1970. These animals came to the shelter with an advantage over strays, because in most cases, the owner could provide a history of the pet. But many of these dogs, cats and other creatures were old or sick; essentially, these owners were bringing their pets in to have them euthanized.

Young animals held a further advantage over the senior pets. Strays were held for a minimum of six days in order to give owners a chance to claim them. After that, the strays were put into the general adoption pool. OHS reported in 1970 that the number of adoptions had doubled—but the number of unwanted animals also had increased. Indeed, the Society put out a bulletin in 1972 declaring: "Hundreds of puppies, dogs, kittens and cats are available to select from. Quite often hamsters, rabbits, white rats, fish, birds, monkeys, pet raccoons and many other good pets are awaiting a new owner.

For those who are looking for a larger pet, the Society often receives horses, sheep, goats, turkeys, ducks, chickens and other barnyard animals that need new homes."

For more than a century, OHS has helped families find homes for unwanted pets.

Cuddling their new dog Lucy in Best Friends' Corner, Debbie and Peter Burns marked the 11,000th OHS adoption of the year in December 2014.

The move to adoption counseling meant that the counselor could provide information on pet care to prospective owners and also advise them on pet compatibility to make sure the owners were getting a pet they could live with for the rest of its life. Adoption counselors also helped with adjustment issues as pets moved into their new homes.

Still, some prospective adopters complained about what they called onerous adoption procedures. In 1993, a consultant came in to provide adoption sensitivity training to the staff. "We are working on approach issues because we believe most of our concerns can be fixed by the way we say things," the minutes from a 1993 board meeting stated.

Profile

TERRI ROUSH: GIVING WISE COUNSEL

Terri Roush started working at OHS in August 1990 as an adoption counselor in the old building. "I was totally taken with the grounds," she said. "It looked Southern and charming from the outside. The front was all grass, with oak trees and wisteria covering the walkway." But the minute Roush walked in the office, the charm disappeared.

"The building was incredibly old—very hot in the summer and extremely cold in the winter," she remembered. "The break room inside the building was rustic, with a tree stump standing in the middle of the small room. It had a certain character to it."

Conditions in the old shelter were hardly ideal. "Kennel cough was rampant throughout the open kennels and when we heard dogs coughing on a walk-through inventory, we were required to euthanize them," she said. "Sometimes we were less than honest, rather than see a dog put down."

Back then, the shelter's capacity was 80-85 dogs. It wasn't clean and the ceiling leaked in the adoption office. "On the other side of the small parking lot where Paul Meyers had a maintenance shop, there was the crematorium that also housed records. Staff would retreat to the small out-building because it was warm. We always had the barn and lovely rose garden," she recalled.

For Roush, the biggest change came when the new building opened in 1999. But the leadup to construction was long. Just to show how she and Sharon Harmon felt about the crumbling place where they had been working, when the building was vacated, "Sharon Harmon and I threw rocks at the windows of the old shelter," Roush remembered. "I couldn't throw very well, but Sharon had a pretty good arm."

The change from the creaky old structure to the sparkling new shelter could not have been more dramatic: "It was like moving from a building that barely had indoor plumbing to a five-star hotel."

With the opening of the new building, Roush moved from adoption counseling to full-time retail work as the new store manager for Best Friends' Corner. In a small corner off the main lobby of the new building, she said, "We initially sold food and basic supplies, like leashes, to new adopters. We had to educate adopters on what supplies they needed before taking their new pets home."

Even after she retired from OHS in April 2014, Roush wanted to stay connected. Today she volunteers to help maintain the rose garden. "I could never leave," she said.

Paul Meyers and Terri Roush show awards for the prize-winning OHS rose garden.

FUN FACT
Each year, OHS places more than 11,000 pets in new homes.

Concurrently, in the early 1990s, the Purina Pets for People program began providing free adoptions to about 120 senior citizens per year. Pets for the Elderly Foundation still helps subsidize reduced-cost adoptions by senior citizens.

Adoptions continued to soar. In the first seven months of 1999, OHS placed a record 4,356 animals—a 25 percent increase over the previous year. Executive Director Sharon Harmon credited the increase to programs such as Pet Pals, working with problem dogs and providing temporary homes. Harmon also lauded the greater media attention and improved customer service by staff. She pointed to a greater volunteer presence, more aggressive adoption outreach, more foster homes and more staff. At the Third Annual Adopt a Pet Fair that year, a one-day adoption record was set as 75 animals found new homes. The record was broken in 2007, with an all-time high of 101 pets going home on the day of the OHS Telethon on Nov. 17.

In the case of OHS adoptions, success has continued to breed still more success. Today, most pets adopted through OHS come from a network of more than 90 independent humane societies and rescue organizations throughout the West.

This Second Chance program brings pets from overcrowded shelters elsewhere and finds homes for them. This collaboration with other animal welfare groups goes back to 1995, rooted in the notion that when shelters pool resources such as kennel space and foster homes, everybody wins. Many of the animals transferred to OHS from other shelters were facing euthanasia. At OHS, they found new homes instead. In 1999, OHS added the Kauai Humane Society to the list of its organizational partners. Maui has since joined the list. A partnership with Alaska Airlines allows those pets to receive free transportation from the Hawaiian Islands to Portland.

Benefactor Ellyn Bye joins OHS volunteers at a Second Chance

SHELTER CARE

"Just a Little Love"

~ By Lana Duran

Reprinted from *OHS Magazine*, Fall 1991

A frightened dog sits in his kennel, unaware of his surroundings, not understanding why he is here or who these unfamiliar people are. He is provided with food and water and a warm blanket but still he shakes from uncertainty. Someone comes to his kennel and talks to him. She knows his name and seems friendly enough. Holding his leash, she encourages him to go outside for a walk. Reluctantly he accepts the invitation and leaves his kennel to get to know this new friend.

Every day, OHS employees see a large number of confused and misunderstood animals that were not fortunate enough to have found permanent, loving homes. The owners of these animals have usually done their best to try placing their pet in a good home, but when they were unable to do so they turned to us for help.

During an animal's stay at the shelter, our employees and volunteers will do many things to help it feel secure and comfortable. It is very important that the animal remain socialized and accepting of this change in lifestyle so that it will have an easy transition to a new home when chosen for adoption.

For some animals, comfort and security may mean a familiar toy that was brought along with them, for others it's a friendly person sitting in the kennel talking, petting and reassuring it. Many animals bond quickly with the person who first takes it out of the kennel for a walk or a game of fetch. A badly matted dog may find security in the one who takes the time to bathe him and remove the tangles and clumps that have burdened him for months. Many animals that we receive have been left outside for most of their lives with little more than food or water. It can be difficult and time consuming for us to win their trust, but for these animals we offer our love, understanding and patience, and we hope that time will heal their insecurities.

FUN FACT

OHS dog walking volunteers use upwards of 1,000 compostable poop bags a week.

Our spacious and colorful Second Chance vehicles bring pets from elsewhere in Oregon and around the West to find new homes through OHS.

24

Find that Animal!

Animal licenses were introduced by the City of Portland in 1855. Almost from its founding, OHS kept hand-written records of lost pets in giant ledger books.

This practice continued until county agencies took over the work. A separate ledger kept track of people hoping to adopt unusual breeds of cats or dogs. People who called in to find out if a lost pet had found its way to OHS were told to come on out and take a look. But this was not so easy for people without cars. Even the city bus stopped almost a mile from the shelter. In 1967, a board member named Mrs. Fields urged the OHS workers who were going out each morning to pick up animals around the city to read lost and found columns from city newspapers.

In the 1930s, it was not uncommon to use the "identacode" method of marking dogs. Usually used for pedigreed dogs, this consisted of tattooing an animal with a mark that was recorded on both the pedigree and the certificate of ownership. Fifty-plus years later, OHS began offering laminated plastic tags for $5. One side was engraved with OHS information and the phone number 228-FIND, along with a tag number. In turn that information was registered in the OHS database, enabling anyone who found a pet with an OHS tag to obtain contact information about the owner.

OHS went high-tech in 1983, with a computerized lost and found system to help owners find pets in a matter of seconds. In 1986, the Lost Pet Helpline was so busy that staffing it had become a full-time position. Each day in 1986, OHS received reports of about 50 lost and found animals.

Today, stray animals are directed to county animal services agencies as the one place to help them find their way home.

Around 1992, microchips implanted subcutaneously, near a pet's shoulder blades, augmented tags, which still remain the most reliable means of tracing a pet. The chip contains information needed to locate an owner. A scanner reads the chip, providing another method of recovering a pet. By 2001, all animals adopted from OHS were microchipped. They were also spayed or neutered—including dogs, cats and rabbits.

when Oregon was still a territory, the City of Portland issued animal licenses printed by *The Oregonian*.

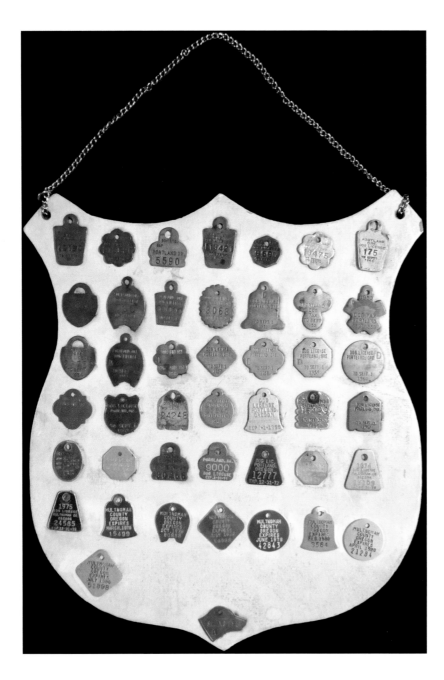

Visible identification, like these dog license tags, is the most effective way to ensure a lost pet is returned home.

25

Meow

Oh, to be a kitty at OHS!

A 1976 gift from the Oregon Cat Fanciers allowed OHS to remodel its Cat Haven. Now the felines had shelves to scale, a tree to climb and toys to play with. The glassed-in kitty oasis made it easy for visitors and OHS workers to observe all the feline fun. Those lucky cats got a constant supply of fresh water from automatic water bowls. Young cats were separated from the older, potentially more aggressive cats.

'39 shelter featured a cozy cattery for felines.

A project called "Pet Pride of Oregon" became associated with OHS in 1980, with the goal of promoting cat welfare programs and activities. The project also encouraged spaying, and in one year alone, accounted for a 25 percent increase in the number of cat adoptions.

As was the case for shelters everywhere, summer at OHS was known as "kitten season." Executive Director Sharon Harmon said in 1992 that the influx of cats was sometimes overpowering. "For the past 18 years, I dreaded this [summer] season because of the overwhelming numbers of animals that ended up at animal shelters," Harmon said. "Kitten season with its endless boxes, laundry baskets, milk crates, etc., of baby cats, mostly perfect but too many, many sick with no chance, lined up at the receiving room door taxing one's patience with humanity. You could see the effect on the staff and volunteers— haggard, burnt out. Those of us working in the trenches fighting pet overpopulation and uncaring pet owners feel the effects of the season personally and professionally."

The growing influx of cats was one reason why, in 1999, Harmon began urging a new shelter to save more cats. "All the policy changes, foster homes, TLC offered by our dedicated staff and volunteers cannot change the fact that there is not enough room to care for all the cats brought to our old shelter," she argued. "Once they are here, the old shelter harbors disease and is so stressful for our feline friends that they get sick despite our best efforts. More than any other measure of success, the new shelter will allow us to save thousands more lives every year because of the amount and quality of space for cats."

Cattery accommodations in the old days were less than luxurious.

Individual kennels and colony rooms showcase cats and kittens in today's shelter.

26

Not Just Cats and Dogs

Dogs and cats account for the bulk of OHS adoptions, but about 10 percent of the animals adopted each year are rabbits, rodents and birds.

A 1995 donation from Phil Paradis, the regional manager of Petco, provided the seed money for a new Rabbit and Rodent Room, housing the increasing numbers of rabbits, guinea pigs, gerbils, hamsters, rats, mice and bunnies that were coming in. Four years later, a group of bunny-loving OHS volunteers dubbed themselves the Rabbit Advocates, dedicated to educating people about rabbits as well as encouraging rabbit fostering and adoption.

Birds of all feathers find homes through OHS.

Larger critters also find homes and legislative champions through OHS. Livestock surfaced as an OHS priority as early as 1882, when OHS President David Thompson, also the mayor of Portland, advocated that "In view of the coming railroads and attendant transportation of cattle, the society should call upon the next legislature to enact stringent laws for their proper protection."

Nearly a century later, OHS conducted a 1966 investigation following a report of nearly 500 undernourished cows on Saddle Mountain in Harney County, near Burns. They determined that the reports were false, and that bad blood between stockmen had produced the original complaint.

At a meeting with the board in 1992, Society Director Dale Dunning raised the sensitive topic of soring horses. The practice of treating the hooves of Tennessee Walker horses with acid or another substance that causes pain when the animals' hooves touch the ground has long been employed as a means to make the horses lift their hooves higher. High-stepping, as this equine action is known, makes the animals appear to be dancing, almost as if in a chorus line. Dunning wanted to protect animals in Oregon from this cruel treatment, but his efforts for a statewide ban did not succeed. In 2006, soring became illegal in the United States. But with no criminal sanctions, the practice continued. As late as 2017, bills were pending in Washington and Salem to criminalize this barbaric act.

Small animals such as this rabbit
and white rat make great pets,
this Telethon guest agrees.

What a busy barnyard.

A wild burro from Death Valley National Monument who was rescued from a Central Oregon meat packing plant in 1995 joined the residents in the OHS barn. Back then, recued barnyard animals lived in an historic barn behind the current shelter that was known as a "Lollypop Farm." City children came to visit and learn about farm animals. The animals, to make a bad pun, were even something of a cash cow for OHS. In June, 1964, board minutes noted that "the sheep had been sheared and the wool sold for $65."

BARN FOR ANIMALS VOTED

Humane Society to Build Shelter Near Its Kennels.

A barn to shelter animals will be built at once in the four-acre pasture owned by the Oregon Humane society adjacent to its kennels on Columbia boulevard, directors of the organization voted at their meeting yesterday. It will cost approximately $900.

Plans for National Humane week, April 16 to 21, were discussed. Permission will be requested from the school board to conduct a poster contest in the schools and winning posters would be submitted in the national contest.

P. M. Baldwin, president, presided. Mrs. Charles T. Hoge and Robert Mish, new directors, attended for the first time. Charles Rude assumed the duties of treasurer.

Plans for the barn were announced in February 1928

Wool from these sheep helped pay the bills at OHS in 1964.

Chickens and goats were among the residents of the Lollypop Farm.

The Old Red Barn, as it was also known, held horses, baby lambs, pigs, chickens, ducks and other farm animals. Along with a spacious pasture, there was a small lake, where ducks and geese could take their babies for a first swimming lesson.

Today, the barn is used largely for storage. Barnyard animals brought to OHS are fostered out to facilities better able to provide care, such as Sound Equine Options. The pond provides a lovely portion of the naturescaped dogwalking path, complete with visiting wildlife.

In recent years, OHS has restored the pond near the Old Barn to provide attractive habitat for native species.

28

Legislation & Legal Affairs

In the field of animal protection and animals rights legislation, Oregon has been a true paragon. Since its very inception, OHS has been a steady, driving force in the push to establish sound animal protection laws.

"Whenever someone has said there ought to be a law against it, you can be sure a Humane Society advocate was drafting one."
~ 1995 *OHS Annual Report*

Laws protecting animals in this country date back to the Pilgrims. In 1641, when animals were generally viewed as objects or possessions to be used or abused at the will of their owners, the Pilgrims enacted "The Body of Liberties." Among these 100 rights, number 92 was "OFF THE BRUITE CREATURE: No man shall exercise any Tiranny or Crueltie towards any bruite Creature which are usuallie kept for man's use."

Now flash forward a few centuries to Portland, 1868. Keep in mind just how new this Wild West region was when Section (2) of Ordinance No. 241 was enacted as "An Ordinance to provide for the Taxing and Killing of Dogs." With amendments, the bill read: "The owner or person having in charge any dog permitted to run at large within the City limits, shall on or before the first day of September of each year pay into the City Treasurer the sum of Two Dollars and fifty cents in gold or silver coin for each and every dog which shall entitle him to an receipt from the Treasurer, designating the owner name and the number of the license, which number shall correspond with that worn by the dog."

March ahead to 1872. A noble effort by Rep. J. F. Caples (R-Multnomah) to pass a bill in the Oregon Legislature banning animal cruelty fell to defeat. Oregonians are not only hardy, but also persistent. The following year, the City of Portland did ordain as follows: "Section 1. Any person who shall cruelly beat, torture, misuse, deprive of food or water, or otherwise treat any animal with cruelty, shall upon conviction before the Police Judge be deemed guilty of a misdemeanor, and be punished by a fine of not less than five nor more than one hundred dollars, or by imprisonment in the City Jail not exceeding twenty days, or both fine and imprisonment at the discretion of the Police Court."

Section 2 went further still, decreeing: "One half of any fine collected for a violation of Section one (1) of this ordinance shall be paid by the Police Judge to the person making the complaint for his own use of the use of any Society he may represent."

By 1884, OHS was successful in getting Oregon's first statewide animal cruelty law passed. The following year, Oregon legislators passed a basic humane law "for more effective prevention of cruelty to animals." The bill carried stiff punishments: "Whoever overdrives, overloads, deprives of necessary sustenance, cruelly beats, mutilates or cruelly kills, shall for every offense be punished by imprisonment in the county jail not exceeding 60 days or by fine not exceeding $100 or by both fine and imprisonment."

More measures aimed at thwarting animal cruelty. OHS Board Member Robert Tucker took it upon himself in 1915 to send Portland's mayor a draft of an ordinance requesting the legal means "to stop the disreputable proceedings known as cock fighting." A prominent Portland businessman and OHS board member named

In 1973, OHS proposed a new law to spell out a working definition of animal cruelty. The effort to prohibit steer-busting continued, and another bill proposed that a portion of dog license funds be set aside for emergency veterinary care of injured or sick stray dogs.

A proposal in 1974 to set a limit of two dogs and two cats per household proved unpopular. The board had better luck with a 1979 measure forbidding the sale and use of snare and leghold traps. In 1980, OHS was instrumental in obtaining laws making animal fights illegal. OHS also supported a 1982 Portland city ordinance providing, essentially, equal rights for cats. It seemed that few jurisdictions included cats within animal protection laws. OHS investigations had shown that cats given away free frequently were sick or injured, or were subject to mistreatment. One year later, Multnomah County also took up the kitty cause, enacting a cat registration program. OHS officials testified that mandatory registration would save the lives of thousands of cats who otherwise would be euthanized each year.

Executive Director Dale Dunning was off to the heartland in 1990 to lecture at the first-ever National Cruelty Investigations School. This program, initiated by the University of Missouri Extension, offered a course in specialized veterinary and law enforcement training. Dunning continued to teach at the school annually, and by 1994 he had passed his knowledge of animal welfare on to 500 participants from 400 agencies throughout the United States.

OHS also helped craft a 1991 measure intended to make it difficult for research facilities to acquire pets without the owners' knowledge of where the animal was actually headed. OHS offered plaudits the same year to two state legislators who introduced a bill making sexual assault of animals a crime with a felony penalty. The society

backed a 1993 initiative to stop bear baiting and hound hunting of cougars and bears. Getting this bill on the ballot meant gathering the signatures of almost 68,000 Oregon voters. By 1994, the measure became law.

HB3377, the Aggravated Animal Abuse bill, making the malicious killing or torture of animals in Oregon a Class C felony, went into effect on September 9, 1995. Just seven days later OHS received a call from a Milwaukie woman who said her kids had found a decapitated cat bound with duct tape in the field next to their apartment complex. The following morning, after OHS had begun an investigation, another woman called to report a cat found in similar condition. A check with Gladstone police turned up two more cases, but no leads. With the help of tipsters who came forward after coverage on KATU, one adult and several juvenile offenders were charged, with the adult receiving jail time for their offense.

That dreadful case was followed by another new law allowing shelters holding seized animals to petition the court for a disposition hearing. When abuse is established, the court can order the defendant to post a bond equal to the cost of care from the date of seizure to trial date, or forfeit the animals to the holding facility.

Not all the legislative efforts succeeded. A 1997 spay-neuter measure was defeated, but an important bill empowering veterinarians to report animal abuse passed. OHS also helped defeat a swath of repressive bills, including efforts to resume hound-hunting of cougars and bears and a bill from the live-pet lobby that sought to stifle reporting of animal abuse in pet stores. OHS also played a role in quashing a "poaching promotion" measure intended to legalize the sale of wildlife parts. On the county level, OHS assisted in the creation of a special prosecutor program empowering attorneys to assist overworked district attorneys in the prosecution of crimes against animals.

There is a real sense that progress is being made, that values are changing.

~ 1997 *OHS Annual Report*

It took some wrangling, but the greater Portland area finally broke with the traditional shoot-on-sight view of coyotes. A leader in this move was Portland International Airport, which agreed to use non-lethal control methods. In October 1997, Lake Oswego residents strongly supported living with wildlife rather than exterminating it. OHS continues to advance this respectful, humane philosophy.

Legislative progress advanced in 1999 with the passage of an OHS-supported bill eliminating the automatic death penalty for dogs who kill or wound livestock. With a schedule of progressive civil penalties and remedial measures established, offending animals also were required to be microchipped for permanent identification. OHS sponsored a bill passed the same year specifying that animals kept as pets did not automatically become part of the estate when an owner dies, and instead allowing a family member, friend or animal shelter to take immediate custody or place the pet in a suitable home. It also became a crime in 1999 to deal in fur products made from domestic cats or dogs if the fur is obtained through a process that maims or kills the animal.

But despite the Society's best lobbying efforts, a 1999 bill that would have banned "canned" hunting ranches that promote unsportsman-like practices failed to pass. Another OHS-supported bill that failed that year would have prohibited carrying an animal in the external part of a vehicle in certain circumstances. OHS opposed a 1999 bill that, had it passed, would have mandated an experimental cougar harvest program for certain parts of the state.

As the new century dawned, OHS banded with a broad coalition of animal welfare groups working toward a ban on leghold traps along with two wildlife poisons. In the 2001-2002 legislative session, OHS successfully petitioned to be included on Oregon's state tax form, allowing tax filers to designate a portion of their tax refund to OHS.

With strong support from OHS, Oregon became one of the first states to end the use of small and inhumane battery cages to confine hens. On June 17, 2011, Gov. John Kitzhaber signed the landmark legislation that required Oregon egg producers to invest an estimated $65 million over 15 years to phase in an "enriched colony system" of hen housing. The bill meant a revolution in the poultry world, ensuring that hens once housed in cramped, dirty cages would have enough room to stand up, turn around, spread their wings and have access to perches, nesting boxes and scratching areas.

"This legislation will set a new bar for animal welfare by enacting, for the first time, comprehensive animal care standards for hens," said Sharon Harmon, executive director of OHS. "Oregon is a national leader on this issue."

Ironically, the same measure that OHS worked so hard to see enacted was opposed by the Humane Society of the United States (HSUS). But just weeks after the hen-care bill was signed into law, HSUS abruptly withdrew plans for ballot initiatives in Oregon and Washington that advocated a "cage free" system mandating minimum space requirements for hens, but little else. (OHS is not affiliated with HSUS.)

"We're glad that HSUS has seen the light and is now joining the Oregon Humane Society in supporting a comprehensive standard of care represented by our state's new law," Harmon said. "In Oregon, animal advocates and businesses worked together to find a solution to the terrible conditions many hens are subjected to."

Also in 2011, OHS backed new a new law that streamlined the process for abandoned animals at vet clinics, allowing them to be adopted faster. Another new law in 2011 authorized district attorneys to seek forfeiture of animals believed to have been abused, thus allowing them to placed in adopted homes. Any person convicted of sexual assault of an animal was now required to be reported as a sex offender under another 2011 law backed by OHS. Recognizing that spouses may be hesitant to seek a restraining order from an abusive partner if they know their pets may be subject to possible abuse, OHS fought for a 2011 law authorizing courts to provide for the safety of animals when issuing restraining orders. Finally, as concerns mounted over the decline in shark populations, OHS backed a 2011 law that prohibits Oregonians from possessing or selling shark fins.

OHS was also at the forefront in 2013 when state legislators enacted SB6, the Omnibus Animal Bill. Thanks to strong leadership by Senate President Peter Courtney, the sweeping new measure recognized animals as sentient beings under state law, while providing stiffer fines and punishment for convictions on charges of animal neglect.

A 2014 measure in Salem drew strong support from OHS Executive Director Sharon Harmon, who feared that easing the definition of an animal welfare organization could lead to trouble. Harmon stated that "In the last decade there has been a tremendous increase in the underground pet railroad. There are thousands of animals moving through these nontraditional groups in Oregon...these rescues fly under the radar in every sense. The phenomenon of animal rescue turned hoarder is not too far down the road for many of these groups."

During every legislative session, OHS works to strengthen legal protections for animals. Sometimes, help comes from unexpected sources. In June 2017, Harmon said she was nearly upstaged by a trio of poised, articulate Girl Scouts who testified in support of a measure that now allows citizens to break into a motor vehicle if an unattended child or animal is at risk, with no civil or criminal liability for the Good Samaritan. OHS also stepped in to advance the fight against the blood sport of cock fighting. Previous rules allowed authorities only to seize animals directly involved in the fights. The 2017 refinements to the bill permit law enforcement to seize all animals on the premises, regardless of whether they were directly participating in fights. OHS also worked to pass a 2017 law extending the period in which people convicted of certain crimes against animals are banned from owning animals.

Investigations

Even the toughest animal protection laws can't be enforced without thorough investigations to determine when and where abuse or neglect is taking place.

As early as 1882, OHS President David P. Thompson, also the mayor of Portland, praised the humane officers who looked into suspected brutality cases. "Although unostentatious, the officers have inquired into quite a number of cases of cruelty, both to animals and to children, and have effected the necessary amelioration, or secured punishment of offenders," Mayor Thompson reported.

But animal welfare advocates needed help in getting their message out. While enforcing animal cruelty laws in 1884, Officer Felix Martin quickly realized that education would play a key role in protecting animals from abuse and neglect. In a letter to OHS he stated, "The work of this society is new to the people of this city and surrounding country and before enforcing the law governing this matter, the community should be educated so that the objects and aims of the society might be fully understood."

George H. Himes, then the OHS secretary, distributed a pamphlet in 1895 that contained a summary of state anti-cruelty laws, as well as the constitution and bylaws of OHS. This tradition continues to this day, with OHS providing animal law booklets to police officers and sheriff's deputies statewide.

That same year, Thomas Lamb Eliot presented an address at the OHS annual meeting called "To Aid Humane Work." Eliot reminded his audience that while the society often received requests for help with abuse situations from other counties, OHS only had jurisdiction

Col. E. Hofer, first volunteer officer, Oregon Humane Society, worked to enforce laws for prevention of cruelty.

Gary Kish and Sharon Harmon joined the OHS Investigations team to celebrate the purchase of a new truck in 1990.

at that time within the City of Portland. To this day, OHS continues Eliot's practice of urging that "every justice of the peace" in the state be given a copy of state laws about cruelty and neglect. "Complaints of cruelty and neglect of animals may be laid by any one," Eliot pointed out, "and arrests, without warrants, can be made by any officer."

By 1909, Portland Police Chief Gritzmacher was issuing this directive to police captains: "Instruct the officers of your respective commands to give better attention to the matter of preventing cruelty to animals." Gritzmacher said he had heard that some officers "give no heed whatever to offenders of this kind." Indeed, he continued, "Officers have been seen standing on street corners and teamsters going by

driving lame and decrepit horses and no effort made by the officers whatever to interfere or even remonstrate with the drivers on behalf of the dumb animals."

Gritzmacher admonished that officers who failed to take action "are not doing their duty." He added, "The fact that some officer is detailed especially for this kind of work does not relieve any police officer from looking after cases of cruelty to animals." And just in case any confusion remained, Gritzmacher stressed that "for humanity's sake" his order did not refer only to horses, "but to every animal."

A dog gets a ride with Asst. Chief M. Laudenklos & Batt. Chief B. F. Dowell in front of Portland City Hall

No one can know whether the officers who arrested eight men on charges of cruelty to animals in 1911 were spurred by Gritzmacher's charge. Patrolman Mallon took in the eight men at the corner of Fifteenth Avenue and Washington Street. As evidence, Mallon took in 16 horses and mules with sore necks and shoulders. In court, Mallon testified that he saw the men beating the animals because they could not pull their heavy loads. A second investigating officer said four horses should have been used to pull the loads that the men were attempting to haul with two.

Awareness about animal cruelty gradually grew. OHS was called upon to investigate a report of a dog with a broken leg in 1915, and in 1922, the Humane Officer was dispatched to Ochoco National Forest following reports of starving livestock there.

Recalling its early mission of looking out for the welfare of animals and children, in 1943 OHS was called on to investigate a case of child neglect in Hillsboro. With the help of Washington County's district attorney and sheriff, "the children were put under good care and the case otehwise settled following several trips," notes from the case report. Meantime, in 1944, the Humane Officer uncovered a worrisome case of dog poisoning, apparently by strychnine. Twenty years later, OHS looked into a case of 10,000 chickens left for several days without food or water.

ROBBERY!

Manuel Hudson was just doing his job, running the vacuum cleaner, when two, perhaps three robbers broke into OHS in 1964. They threw a cover over his head, tied him up and placed him in the isolation ward. Then they dug open the safe and stole about $180 from the petty cash drawer. They also broke open the donation bottle, which contained about $40 and $15 worth of stamps. Just two months later, masked men once again broke in through a window, restrained the hapless Mr. Hudson and absconded with $753. The board decided to purchase a new safe from Portland Safe Company and deemed it necessary for the bookkeeper to deposit funds nightly at the bank.

"Mr. Zimmer called attention to quick justice given a dog beater by Judge Edmond Jordan recently. Officer witnessed a man beating his dog unmercifully, he said. The officer swore out a warrant for Carl Richardson on a cruelty charge. Judge Jordan fined the man $25 if he would sign a release on the dog—otherwise the fine would have been larger. The release was signed and the dog, a pitiful little mutt, was adopted by a court attache", Mr. Zimmer said.

~ OHS Board Minutes, March 15, 1966

In 1965, OHS investigated 37 abuse/neglect complaints in April alone. July and August, with hot sun beating down, brought 22 neglect investigations, mostly dogs with no food or water. The next year a Portland resident who had seen pictures in *Life* magazine of animals in "Concentration Camps for Dogs" in Maryland and Oklahoma called to express concerns about a house at 19th Avenue and Pettygrove Street where he had heard dogs whining and barking. An OHS investigation found about 40 dogs, some of whom showed signs that they were being used for experimentation.

In 2015, a new era in law enforcement began as Humane Special Agents at OHS were for the first time commissioned by the Superintendent of Oregon State Police. Until then, OHS investigators received their police authority from a direct commission by Oregon's Governor. However, these commissions lacked stability: a change in the occupant of the Governor's mansion could change the officers' status. As Sharon Harmon noted at the time, "By bringing OHS agents under the authority of the state police, the legislature has recognized the importance of fighting animal crime today and long into the future." OHS agents are authorized to enforce animal cruelty laws throughout the state, and must meet the same standards of professional training and conduct that Oregon has established for every certified police officer.

Today, OHS is known as the one place in the state capable of handling large-scale rescues, and works with law enforcement on cases involving 100 or more cats or dogs several times each year. But OHS is committed to humane treatment of all animals. In 2014, Sharon Harmon spoke out when William Holdner and Jane Baum were convicted of 122 counts in the neglect of 170 cattle in what had been the one of the state's longest, most complex animal cruelty cases. A joint investigation by OHS and the Columbia County Sheriff's office had found the animals severely malnourished. Many also suffered from eye infections or other diseases. Holdner and Baum were fined $100,000, placed on five years' probation and barred from owning livestock for the term of their probation.

"The jury's verdict," Harmon stated, "leaves no doubt that owners who fail to provide food and medical care for their animals will face criminal penalties."

Sometimes the carrot of a reward encourages witnesses to animal crime to come forward. In March 1948, "the society re-affirmed its standing reward of $250 for information leading to arrest and conviction of dog poisoners." That April, "[Board member] Smith told of a Hillsboro man having made claim to the reward of $250 for furnishing evidence that caused arrest and conviction of a dog poisoner—the victim being the informant's own dog."

To encourage public awareness of animal neglect, the board voted in 1967 to maintain a revolving reward fund of not less than $1,000 for information "leading to the arrest and conviction of persons perpetrating extreme cruel acts upon live animals." Horrified at the brutal killing of "Donner," a German shepherd belonging to the executive director of the Humane Society of Central Oregon, Howard Hedinger revived the fund in 2000. The trick with a reward fund is setting the amount high enough to motivate witnesses who can assist in the arrest and conviction of guilty abusers, but not so high as to attract those merely interested in the bounty. Rewards of $1,000 to $5,000 have been offered for clues to a 2003 series of dog poisonings in Laurelhurst Park; for a tiny kitten whose tail, ears and whiskers were cut off in 2000; and in a Washington County case of ducks and geese being injured by blow darts.

Profile
HOWARD HEDINGER: TO THE RESCUE

He was just a kid, maybe 13 or 14, when his dad brought him down to the shelter to find a new pet. There were no fancy pet boutiques in Portland back then, no purveyors of designer dog breeds or vendors of costly accessories for Fido or Fifi.

"See, in those days, that was all you thought of," Howard Hedinger remembered of his first trip to the Oregon Humane Society more than 60 years ago. "That was it."

The place was small and crowded, "probably the size of this room, that was it, that was the Humane Society," he said. The first dog Howard and his father saw was scheduled soon for euthanasia, standard practice in that long-ago era. She was large and pregnant, a shepherd mix with soulful eyes.

"So my dad said, 'we'll take the dog,'" Hedinger said. They named her Sherry. Most of her pups went to friends and neighbors, but Howard kept two of them. They lived by his side for the next 16 years. In fact, at 80, Hedinger could not recall a time when he didn't have dogs in his life. A dog lived with him at his fraternity at the University of Oregon. Once, while on a business trip in California, a Great Dane followed him back to his motel. Hedinger posted lost-dog notices, and when no one responded, the Dane went home to Oregon with him.

"Babe, we called him," he said of the sleek Harlequin Dane who joined his family for the next 14 years—a remarkable run for such a large animal.

(Continued on next page)

(Continued from previous page)

If animals in Oregon could have a cosmic godfather, it would be Howard Hedinger. This powerful business leader has a legendary soft spot for every animal on the planet. His personal mission is to make sure they are healthy, safe and loved. For Hedinger, it's personal when anyone harms an animal. When blow darts were injuring water fowl, Hedinger stepped forward to personally offer rewards to bring the perpetrators to justice. When a huge rescue strained the resources of the Oregon Humane Society, Hedinger worked with OHS to post a challenge on Facebook, asking others to match his gift, and his determination to help care for the rescued animals. Hedinger's success as a businessman belies his huge and open heart for those less powerful, whether hospitalized children or abused and abandoned animals.

"You're always my first person to call," OHS CEO Sharon Harmon told Hedinger as the two discussed their loathing for animal abusers.

But sometimes, his love for animals has had its downside. As a young man, fresh out of the military, he packed his three dogs into his station wagon and took them everywhere with him. This made it "awful tough" for the handsome young bachelor to find a date. "Nobody wanted to ride in the car with me," he said, laughing.

But romance finally triumphed, and Hedinger passed his passion for pooches on to his own children. "My son is a big animal lover," he said, bursting with pride. "He has three dogs at home." As if he were boasting about some rare genetic gift, he added: "He got that from me."

Dogs may be Hedinger's favorite creatures, but horses come close and as a matter of fact, there really isn't an animal he wouldn't rush to defend. Hedinger once challenged a New York heart surgeon who made a prominent display of the skin of a jaguar he had slain. After they had had dinner, Hedinger told the doctor his opinion of the skin splayed atop the doctor's piano.

"He was a hunter—he had taken his bride on a hunting honeymoon, can you imagine that?—and he said, 'well it helps the economy' or something like that. I said, 'no, it doesn't,' and the conversation went downhill from there."

Another time, Hedinger woke up to a front-page article in *The Oregonian* about a herd of starving horses in rural Oregon. The rancher could not afford to feed them, and the local sheriff had granted permission to shoot the horses. Hedinger got on the phone and arranged to have a helicopter send food to the hungry animals. He also sent a truck full of hay.

"We saved the herd," he said. In gratitude, "they named a horse after me, Howie."

Hedinger takes his dogs with him to hospitals and nursing homes. At least one dog often accompanies him to church, making his pet a kind of rock star for Sunday school kids.

His loyalty to OHS is unflagging, as is generosity. "It's a lot different from the old days," he mused. "They're local and they help anyone. The staff is excellent, good people—especially the kids in the front area, the ones you see when you first come in. They're very impressive." Asked what might be improved, Hedinger pauses and then shakes a head full of leonine white hair. "I think it's all going in the right direction."

Hedinger dismisses a compliment about how good he has been to OHS. "Well," he responds, 'You've been good to me." And here, finally, is his advice for OHS as it marks its 150th year: "Keep going the way you're going."

OHS held workshops for investigations and other humane workers at which 23 agencies in Oregon were represented in 1975. Still, obstacles to full enforcement of anti-cruelty regulations persisted. Over and over, attempts to establish humane officers as peace officers were vetoed in Salem. In 1989, Sharon Harmon cautioned, "Society Investigators still receive commissions from the Governor, but the lack of peace officer status is a hindrance to our investigations staff."41

Lacking a full-time investigator, OHS Director Alan Thomas in 1986 named funding this position as one of his top five priorities. But by 1989, it was OHS itself that was the subject of an investigation. Apparently, animal rights activists had been using OHS pharmaceuticals to euthanize thousands of stray dogs and cats they trapped. These groups would sneak into OHS at night and give the stray animals lethal doses of sodium pentobarbital. Unfortunately, no one was checking to see if the animals had owners who might be looking for them. When the story came to light, the OHS board hired a management consultant who discovered that quantities of the drug had gone missing. Many staff members were fired, several board members resigned, and OHS began the process of reinventing itself.

Special fund raising from 1990-1991 allowed OHS director Dale Dunning to re-establish the OHS investigations unit. In May, 1991, during Be Kind to Animals Week, a combined blessing of the animals and unveiling of the new investigations truck took place. The ceremony also marked the introduction of the cruelty and abuse investigations program. According to a report in the Fall 1991 *OHS Magazine*, newly hired Humane Officer Sue Klages' cases included: investigating the care of the horses at Portland Meadows during a recent crisis, rescuing a Canada goose that had been injured by a dog, and working for two desperate hours in the crawl space under a house to rescue a trapped cat. She was at the time the only full-time humane investigator in Oregon.

Sadly, animal mistreatment continued. A report from August, 1992, showed that pending investigations cases included assistance to Josephine County Humane Society, a cat shooting, and pet store

A special patch identified Oregon Humane Society investigators.

trading in wildlife. OHS director Dale Dunning worried in July 1992 about "the scope of the cock fighting problem in Oregon and elsewhere."

OHS supported a law passed in 1991 that used the doctrine of "theft by deception" to clamp down on unscrupulous animal dealers. The first people to be charged under the new law were Brenda Linville, a member of the janitorial staff at the Department of Motor Vehicles, and David and Tracy Stephens of D & T Kennels. Linville made a habit of answering "free to a good home" ads, telling pet owners that she would provide a loving home for animals they could no longer keep. Instead, Linville used the names of people who had recently renewed their drivers' licenses, then conspired with animal dealers to sell the pets for research. OHS joined forces with state and county officials to recover 30 dogs and four cats, reuniting them with their original owners or placing them for adoption. The Oregon Animal Welfare Alliance was among groups that praised OHS as "the one organization properly able to receive and process animals returned from research laboratories and seized from D & T."

One of the rescued dogs was a border collie-Kelpie mix whose auburn coat no doubt inspired his name, Rusty. Rusty went on to contribute to medical science in a different way when he was adopted by OHS volunteer Andrea Wall and trained to become a registered therapy dog. Rusty brought smiles to frail, elderly patients at Providence ElderPlace and was the very first therapy dog to visit Shriner's Children Hospital in Portland. The team was nominated for Pet Partner Team of the Year.

Profile
ANDREA WALL

When Andrea Wall started as a volunteer at OHS in 1983, there was no formal training for volunteers and shelter life was bleak. "Dogs age seven and older were automatically euthanized, as were dogs or cats who were returned to the shelter through no fault of their own," she remembered. "Black animals were first to go, as they were deemed the most unadoptable."

Andrea left OHS to work for Animal Aid. In a single year she helped place more than 100 stockpiled dogs and cats. But when Sharon Harmon became OHS operations director and began vaccinating dogs and cats, Andrea returned to OHS as a volunteer. She supported Harmon's goals of saving more animals and making sure that adopters found the right fit in order to reduce the number of animals who came back to OHS.

The old building was a loud and smelly place, Wall said. Sharp wires stuck out of some kennels so that some dogs scraped their muzzles raw while trying to get out. Dogs sat alone in their cages until the new volunteer exercise program started getting the pups out twice a day.

In talking with prospective adopters, Wall found that many lacked the time, energy or education to care properly for their dogs. She won Harmon's support to develop a pilot project for adoption outreach. Her idea was that OHS volunteers would go off-site with dogs, cats, rabbits and guinea pigs from OHS. The volunteers would distribute spay/neuter coupons, provide information, and collect donations while the public cooed over the shelter animals. But the first outing nearly backfired. Wall arrived at Petco with shelter animals and six volunteers, only to learn that the manager had been fired and his successor knew nothing of the arrangement. One happy placement did come out of that outing: Wall and her husband (and fellow OHS volunteer), Dennis Brown, took home a black Australian Shepherd/

Made for each other: Andrea Wall and Dennis Brown
with their new OHS rescue dog Rusty.

Labrador mix named Jackson to meet their resident dogs. Jackson fit right in and became OHS' first outreach adoption.

Andrea volunteered with OHS' animal assisted therapy program from 1996-2006, training handlers and animals known as pet partners. Andrea had adopted Rusty, a border collie and Kelpie mix, rescuing him from animal medical research, and trained him as a therapy dog. Rusty, who Andrea calls her "heart dog," accompanied her for ten years while she worked as an occupational therapist, specializing in working with seniors in nursing homes and adults in adult day care.

When she brought an Australian Shepherd/Collie mix to an adoption event in the mid-1990s, Wall met Jean Hampel. Hampel directed the Prison Pet Partnership Program in Gig Harbor, Wash., where female inmates trained dogs to be service animals. After training Rusty for therapy assistance work, Wall knew other shelter dogs had the same potential. The Aussie/Collie mix soon joined the prison program, and eventually about 30 shelter dogs were trained at the maximum security prison.

Another shelter dog caught Andrea's attention when she tested a dog named Bridget to do a life-saving job. The Sheltie/Border Collie mix had arrived at OHS pregnant, and with no name. The 14 puppies she delivered were quickly adopted. Something about Bridget made Andrea certain that this dog had special qualities. Andrea tested Bridget to alert for seizures and discovered that Bridget had the sensitivity to smell changes in body chemistry before a seizure episode. Bridget was soon paired with an inmate who suffered from seizures, and later with a Korean War veteran in Richland, Wash. As Wall remembered, "The dog with no name had a job to do."

And then there was the notorious 1993-95 case of Vikki Kittles. This abominable matter prompted a major push by OHS for stricter animal protection laws. Kittles, with her almost demonic ability to work the system in her favor, made it clear how important it was to close every loophole in the law that might protect animal abusers, not animals.

Kittles herself sported a number of pseudonyms—Susan Dietrich, Rene Depenbrock and Lynn Zellan were among them—as she established a decades-long history of animal abuse and hoarding that spanned the country, ranging from the Southeast all the way to the Pacific Northwest. Hers was a textbook profile of animal hoarders, according to the Hoarding of Animals Consortrium (HARC). Some of these traits include:

- **Acquiring animals purely to serve the individual's own needs**

- **Sociopathic characteristics and/or personality disorder**

- **Lack of empathy for people or animals, and extreme indifference to the harm caused either to animals or people**

- **Superficially charming, but extremely manipulative and cunning**

- **Contempt for authority and a determination to beat the system**

Sure enough, Kittles skillfully used a series of legal maneuvers to block authorities from providing medical care or taking custody of the 114 dogs, four cats and two chickens found in her filthy school bus near Astoria to foster homes. "Those animals had to live in cages for 21 months," said Sharon Harmon, then operations director at OHS.

"We literally had to watch some of those dogs die horrible deaths from heart worm. I mean, we could see the worms moving under their skin, and we couldn't do anything for them."

True to the description of hoarding behavior, Kittles was so defiant after she was arrested and placed in a patrol car that she began kicking at the window, forcing a deputy to place her in leg restraints. At trial, Kittles berated the judge, the jurors, the witnesses, the prosecutor and the audience. Contempt charges added 71 days to her sentence. At the time, Oregon law mandated that Kittles could receive no more than a misdemeanor conviction. After a trial that cost taxpayers nearly $1 million, Kittles was sentenced to two years behind bars for animal abuse. Subsequently, a law was enacted to enforce harsher penalties for animal abuse.

"Kittles is in my opinion one of the most dangerous, evil people I have ever encountered," Clatsop County prosecutor Josh Marquis asserted.

OHS garnered national attention in 1994 for assisting in the prosecution of a case involving the alleged abuse by an animal trainer of a two-year-old elephant while performing in a circus in Lebanon, Ore. In 1997, OHS investigators responded to more than 1,000 calls involving everything from neglected wolf hybrids in Clackamas County to cat mutilations in Washington County, to a dog beaten with a bat.

The OHS report noted, "Most importantly, the Investigations Department serves notice that wanton cruelty will not be tolerated."

Over the years, OHS also has done its best to keep a watchful eye on rodeos and other similar events. The Pendleton Round-Up may be a beloved institution to many, but OHS has long been concerned about its toll on animals. With OHS superintendent James Zimmer in attendance, five animals were so badly injured in the steer-busting segment at the 1964 Round-Up that they were quickly taken out and shot. Mr. Zimmer told rodeo officials and Society members alike that he would like to see steer-busting removed from the Round-Up. "It is a poor and cruel sport," Zimmer said soberly. He added that Pendleton was one of only three rodeos in the U. S. —the others were Prineville and Cheyenne—where steer-busting was permitted. An OHS board member concurred, saying he could not understand how "civilized people could enjoy watching animals abused and maimed year after year." The board fired off a letter to the organizers of the Pendleton, Prineville and Cheyenne round-ups, asking that steer-busting be eliminated.

But the practice continued. The following year, Zimmer was in attendance, along with Kenneth McGovern of the American Humane Association, when four steers were injured and had to be destroyed. In 1967, the OHS board learned that Rep. Grace O. Peck had been asked to seek an opinion from Attorney General Bob Thornton as to whether ORS 167740, the cruelty to animals statute, might be applied to control steer-roping contests, or whether another statute would be needed.

The board was equally outraged about the practice of bullfighting, voting in 1966 to oppose any form of bullfighting in Oregon. The board also took aim at the Lil Britches Rodeo, pressing the organizers in 1985 to eliminate the greased pig chase.

Profile
MILAGRO, THE MIRACLE CAT

Strange sounds were emanating from a storage unit in Oregon City in February 2011. The manager called OHS, convinced that what he was hearing was an animal in distress. OHS Humane Officer Austin Wallace rushed the red tabby cat that he found inside the unit to the OHS Holman Medical Center for treatment. The nearly lifeless cat had probably been without food or water for four weeks. The poor kitty was found ensnared in a makeshift leash tied to a shopping cart. Veterinarians were not initially optimistic, but the tabby continued to grow stronger and gain weight. His amazing rebound prompted the medical staff to name him "Milagro," Spanish for miracle. Milagro continued to thrive while being fostered by OHS volunteer Joanne Godfrey, who subsequently adopted him. "Milagro has shown love and affection even though he has been through so much," said Godfrey. "Helping him return to health has given me a sense of purpose in helping those who cannot help themselves."

Meantime, Milagro's original owner, a transient, was located by investigators and charged with criminal animal neglect. He was sentenced to 30 days in jail after entering a guilty plea.

Milagro made a miraculous recovery after being rescued by OHS investigators.

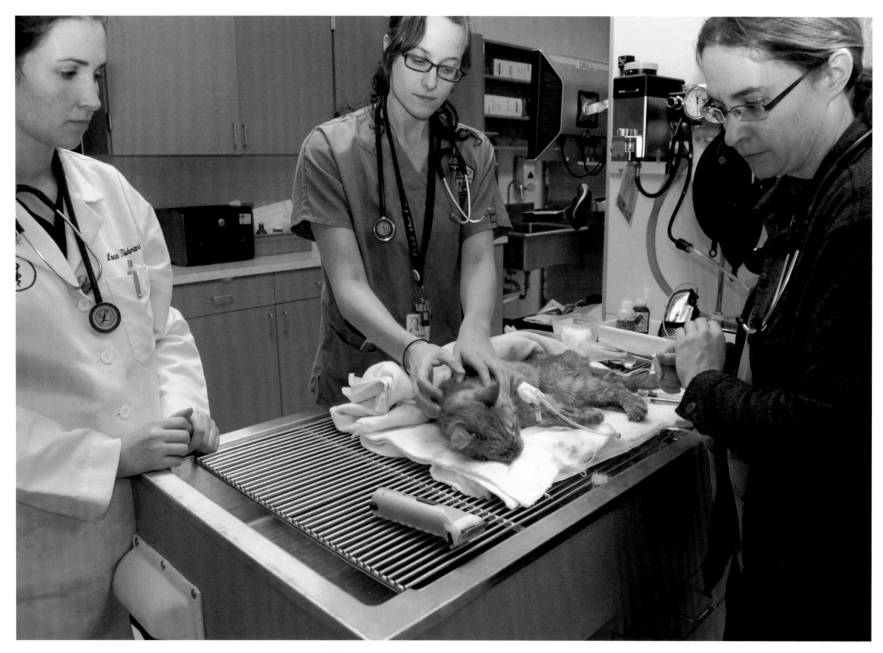

Milagro, rescued by OHS Humane Investigators, is given a new lease on life at the Society's Holman Medical Center.

Sometimes, rescue brings reward. In 1941, the OHS board presented Rodney Krake with $5 after he rescued a springer spaniel who had been struck by a car. While rain plummeted, Krake covered the wounded animal with his own coat while he waited for the OHS ambulance to arrive. Krake, 15, came from what was then known as a broken home. He said nothing about his kindness when he returned that night to the house where he was boarding. The OHS Board also nominated Rodney for an Award of Merit from the American Humane Association and presented him with a $15 savings account, $1 in cash, and a sweater.

Wartime brought renewed alertness, especially with the proximity of the West Coast to Japan during World War II. Just a month after the Japanese attack on Pearl Harbor, OHS trustees urged the society to be "fully prepared to care for a surplus of wounded animals, or lost ones." The Society also made it clear that it stood ready to assist the broader community. Since the OHS building was fireproof, OHS prepared "39 cots in case of war emergency needs." Classes were underway on what to do with animals during air raids.

The attack on Pearl Harbor prompted a rush of people from OHS volunteering for war-related duties. By October of 1942, OHS' Harry Daniel had been appointed director for Oregon of the Red Star Animal Relief, a national effort dating back to WWI to assist animals affected by war. Red Star had been given office space in Civilian Defense headquarters. While much preparedness literature would be mimeographed by the civilian defense committee, the OHS board agreed that covering the cost of additional literature and other expenses" was "in reality a part of the Humane Society's obligation."

This stalwart spaniel was a integral member of the Aircraft Warning Service Observers protecting Portland during World War II.

By April 1943, at least 50,000 booklets on the care of animals during war emergency had been sent around the state. The OHS board of course made patriotic investment decisions as well, purchasing thousands of dollars in war savings bonds with gifts left to the Society in supporters' estates.

Oregonians like Corporal Malcolm R. Herd (right), serving in Guam during World War II, depended on their canine companions.

As the war dragged on, more and more men were drafted, and civilians were called upon to conserve every sort of material for the war effort. One example of how OHS responded took place in July, 1944, when Harry Daniel used plywood to close the cat playroom, both to protect the cats and to aid in fuel conservation.

With the long war at last drawing to a close, OHS wanted to make sure that dogs who had gone to war got the homecoming they had earned. In the fall of 1945, the City Council voted to provide free dog licenses to war dogs for the remainder of their lives. In turn, OHS voted to provide these tags at Society expense. Each round, brass tag would be inscribed with the war dog's name and discharge number. But concern remained. Most returning dogs seemed happy to be back with their owners, but some were less welcoming to strangers. One war dog lunged at the arm of a child waving a toy pistol, and was probably saved from injury—or worse—when the dog's master ordered the dog to "drop it." With concerns mounting that these returning canine heroes might be judged as aggressive—and most likely killed—discussions began to encourage the state legislature to see if accommodations for the dogs could be provided near the veterans' hospital. The dogs could then serve as companions to those in the uniforms they had been taught to protect.

Sometimes we rescue animals; sometimes they rescue us. A five-year-old spayed female dog named Thumper received an OHS medal in 1948 when she rescued her owners from a fire in their Portland home. It seemed that the owners, a couple named LaTosh, had been out late and fell into bed on returning home. About 3 a.m., they awoke to hear Thumper pounding and scratching at their bedroom door. Mr. LaTosh was buff naked when they escaped to the street after quickly calling the fire department. The fire was so intense that Mr. LaTosh's face was blistered and his hair singed. Thumper also suffered injuries to her eyes and ears in the blaze that destroyed the house and the LaToshes' adjacent business. There was no question that the dog had saved her owners' lives.

Disaster Preparedness & Response

Big snowfalls always throw Portland for a loop. This soggy city can cope with rain, but serious snow is another matter. A blizzard in 1943 had OHS officials scurrying to care for their animals. Around the state, much livestock suffered. Some had to be humanely destroyed while others were fed by humane officers.

Floods pose a continuing threat in this rainy region. The still-remembered Vanport floods of 1948 sent more than 100 refugee dogs to OHS from the Vanport area. To keep up with the crisis, OHS operated two rescue wagons on 24-hour duty for the entire week after the floods. A week later, OHS had to move 200 dogs, 60 cats, five goats, 10 sheep and assorted other livestock out to the Gresham fairgrounds, the city zoo and the Multnomah stadium to escape the rising waters. Private kennels also made room for the animals, as did a Portland woman named Margaret Estelle Adams.

Thumper gets a hug from her grateful owner.

A BRIEF HISTORY OF THE ADAMS HOME FOR DOGS

By Lydia Bello

Hiding behind the incinerator at the Oregon Humane Society is a white, wrought iron sign that until about 10 years ago stood over the old OHS kennels. Legend holds that the sign originally identified an organization called the Adams Home for Dogs. The building with the peaked roof at NE Columbia Boulevard and 42nd Avenue, most recently an equipment company, once had a floor plan reminiscent of a kennel. Were the sign and the building once related? And how did the sign end up at the Oregon Humane Society? The story of how the sign came to be at the Humane Society is another chapter in Portland's rich history of animal welfare.

The Adams Home for Dogs at 4123 NE Columbia Boulevard was the legacy of Margaret Estelle Adams, who once operated a small business boarding dogs in the backyard of her Chapman Street home. In her will, Adams stipulated that a trust be established within ten years of her death to continue her work with Portland's canines by "providing for, keeping, maintaining or operating a place/or fund for or for the benefit of stray, homeless or unprovided-for dogs." Her executor and her lawyer, Paul E. Froelich and Alexander G. Barry, did not believe at first that her estate would cover such an ambitious endeavor. To their surprise, they discovered $20,000 in savings, deposited in the bank and in gold coins at her home.

Still, legal and financial complications delayed the opening of the Adams Home for Dogs. Adams' will also included a monthly sum for her sister, with the remainder to go to the home for dogs. When the sister died, Adams' nephew made a claim to the entire estate. But a court ruled against him, and the Adams Home for Dogs was incorporated on March 26, 1937.

Only a few weeks later, the first meeting of the Adams House Trustees convened. A vexing question was the relationship of the new home for dogs with the Oregon Humane Society. Eventually it seemed certain that the Adams House should search for land suitable for an autonomous facility.

In January 1941 a brand-new, "ultra-modern" kennel opened at the intersection of NE 42nd Avenue and Columbia Boulevard with the "latest of sanitary facilities, individual stalls, separate outside runs" and a well-heated interior (*The Oregonian*, January 20, 1941). M. L. Bingham was the insitution's first superintendent, and the Adams House opened with ten dogs.

Unfortunately, the Adams House did not fare well in coming years. Leadership struggles crippled the organization, and finances suffered. Ultimately, the management of Adams House felt that the best move was to join with the Oregon Humane Society, on the condition that OHS designate a portion of its shelter to care for for homeless and stray dogs. There was also the question of the sign. Adams House trustees insisted that there had to be a sign indicating that the property was being maintained through the generosity Margaret E. Adams.

The original Adams Home for Dogs sign was transferred to the Oregon Humane Society with the rest of the corporation's assets, and installed on the property sometime after 1960. Although it is no longer standing and the organization is no longer extant, it still exists as a reminder of the various individuals and organizations that have worked in Oregon alongside the Oregon Humane Society to improve animal welfare.

OHS worked hard to make sure that the pets from Vanport were reunited with their owners. As the waters receded, people who had been washed out visited the shelter to look for their pets. Many had lost everything, but still insisted on taking their dogs with them.

Cats and dogs weren't the only animals OHS harbored during the Vanport floods.

Bitter cold in November, 1964, was followed by Christmas floods. OHS officials worked round-the-clock to rescue pets caught on islands of floating debris in the turbulent waters. At one point, the society housed 130 dogs whose kennels had been swept away. Those recued dogs joined 130 Society-owned dogs that had accumulated after the Christmas giveaway. Out in the society pasture, 33 horses grazed. Two veterinarians, Dr. James L. Adams and Dr. Donald F. Serres of the Oregon City Veterinary clinic, almost lost their lives in the Clackamas River while helping to rescue a horse. In the farming community of Logan, about seven miles from Oregon City, the horse had struggled all day to climb the muddy river bank. The two veterinarians volunteered to swim out to tie a rope around the horse's neck. They managed to pull the horse to safety, but when the men tried to climb the bank, they met the same fate as the horse as the steep, waterlogged bank caved in. They survived, and the OHS Board voted to recommend them for a Stillman Award from the American Humane Association for their heroism.

June Wood's astonishing passel of French poodles occupied a great deal of the Society's time in the fall of 1966. Ninety-nine French poodles were rescued from her dark basement, but four soon died. The remaining 95 required attentive care, including regular administration of oral tablets and feedings of high-protein food mixed with vitamins. The dogs were in bad shape, and on the day of the OHS board meeting in October, 15 were hospitalized.

Board members agreed that rescuing the dogs from the filth and squalor of Mrs. Wood's basement was something that had to be done. They gratefully acknowledged the help that members of the Dog Fancier's Association had provided in coming in to clean the poodles and clip their matted hair, sometimes ingrown into the dogs' flesh. The poodles were definitely receiving the best care they had ever enjoyed. However, the hard truth was that the poodles were taking up a lot of space, time and energy, meaning that some services to the public had had to be curtailed.

Attempts to seek court action had proved fruitless, and Mrs. Wood's attorney also stubbornly refused to accommodate pleas for help from OHS, which by then had become custodian of the dogs for the county. Costs were mounting. Since the dogs' rescue, OHS reported that it had spent at least $1,700—a hefty sum in 1966—to care for the scraggly little poodles.

Mrs. Wood's trial took place on March 9, 1967, nearly five months after the poodles were removed from her basement on SE 52nd Avenue. OHS Director James Zimmer had received board approval to sign a cruelty charge against Mrs. Wood. By the time of the trial, OHS costs in caring for the surviving poodles had soared to at least $2,000.

A jury convicted Mrs. Wood of neglect. But her punishment was light: a suspended sentence and a year's probation. Judge Carl D. Etlinger advised Mrs. Wood to curtail her dog operations, and friends who attended the trial promised to help her maintain better conditions for the dogs. Judge Etlinger added that not only could OHS make regular inspections, but "the court expected the society to do so."

Sadly, Mrs. Wood's poodles went home with her. Three months later, an OHS inspection found the dogs to be in worse condition than when they had first been seized.

"The Society's rescue program is perhaps its most unusual and unpublicized activity," said Executive Director Gene Burgess. "We've rescued everything from rattlesnakes to birds caught in chimneys. We've pulled horses from wells and rescued them from canyons." Fire departments often were too busy to try rescued treed cats, so the job fell to the humane society."

OHS rescue assistance has extended well beyond state borders. At the time that it made landfall in August, 1992, Hurricane Andrew was the most destructive storm in U. S. history. Much of the city of Homestead, Fla., was all but obliterated by Andrew's 165 mile-per-hour winds, making it a Category 5 hurricane—about as damaging as hurricanes can get. In Portland, OHS Director Dale Dunning went right to work on relief efforts, coordinating with the US Army to construct tent cities for people with pets and helping to find foster homes for pets made homeless by the hurricane. In his report to the OHS Executive Committee in September, he noted that American Humane Association, the coordinating agency for animal disaster relief, "has received cooperation from the National Guard in effecting rescues. This dramatic change in policy came as soon as the Federal Emergency Management Agency (FEMA) was relieved of its responsibility for managing the hurricane relief."

A team of OHS staff and volunteers greeted dogs rescued from Hurricane Katrina as they arrived in Portland.

Animal Rescue Team (OHSTAR) were among the first on the scene as animal agencies from around the country came together in an unprecedented effort. During their first three days, the team of four rescued 61 pets, working in toxic flood waters, dripping humidity and 95-degree temperatures to reach pets without guardians, lost, or left at home with dwindling or non-existent supplies of food and water.

Less than a month later, a second storm, Hurricane Rita, worsened the effects of Katrina as it bore down on the Gulf Coast. OHS rescuers in Louisiana helped gather a circle of vehicles around the emergency shelter housing upwards of 12,000 animals, and stayed through the night to protect them. Volunteers were heartened when city officials in Galveston, Tex., announced that pets would be permitted on buses evacuating the low-lying city.

After 13 days in the field, Team One returned to a hero's welcome at OHS, having visited 102 addresses and saved 51 cats, 20 dogs, a hamster, a ferret, two frogs, a tortoise and a rabbit. Marketing Director Barbara Baugnon's mother, who happened to be visiting from New Orleans when the storm hit, cooked up a real Louisiana feast for them, including gumbo, red beans and rice, and all the fixings. Additional teams were deployed from OHS assisting rescue and sheltering efforts, but it became clear that the number of displaced pets exceeded local capacity. In an effort to save lives. OHS staff, board and volunteers struggled to find a means of evacuating some of the pets to Oregon. Success came on October 5, when, through the efforts of board member Jean McNamara, a Continental 737 jet touched down at Portland International Airport with 93 pets aboard.

Then in August, 2005, Hurricane Katrina slammed into the Gulf Coast and New Orleans. Katrina proved to the costliest natural disaster in U. S. history, and one of the country's five deadliest hurricanes up to that time. An estimated 40,000 pets were left behind as desperate humans struggled for their own rescue. Many animals were locked in abandoned homes or chained to fences and porches. Some frightened cats and dogs refused to leave their homes, even as flood waters rose. Volunteers and staff from the OHS Technical

An OHS volunteer's journal from the early days of the operation reads as follows:

Day 4

Our convoy...traveled down the emergency vehicle lane on the freeway heading for New Orleans. Through National Guard and police checkpoints, on and on, until we finally arrived at the destroyed city.

The scene was like a science fiction movie: soldiers armed with automatic rifles roaming the streets in groups; law enforcement vehicles of all sorts (including ours) everywhere, lights flashing; stark military helicopters flying frequently overhead. Downed branches and whole trees are everywhere. Power lines hang low overhead or completely downed and blocking some streets. We drove past houses with roofs blown off and windows broken while some houses appeared untouched. Billboards were torn up by the winds, their crumpled metal legs bent into giant spider creatures.

When we got to the final staging area inside the city, it was very hot. There was a nauseating smell of death that greeted us as we stepped out of our vehicles and into the sweltering day. We were divided into our teams and given a list of addresses where there were known companion animals left by their owners fleeing the hurricane wind and rising waters.

At the end of the day, nearly 6 p.m., we again met at the parking lot staging area where we had started. We transported all the cats to a large pet store in another part of the city, where all the other teams brought their rescued cats, dogs, rabbits, ferrets, birds, and one pot-bellied pig. The animals were seen by a vet or vet tech, and then loaded back into vehicles for the ride to the large staging area's "animal shelter."

It's almost 11 p.m. as I submit this. Unbelievable—at the moment I can't hear any dogs barking! They must all be exhausted, as we all are. We hunkered down in our tents and vehicles to have a bit of rest before heading out again tomorrow.

DAY 5

In spite of the difficulties and nearly every home having barred windows and doors, we were able to rescue 15 cats, 3 dogs, 2 birds, a hamster, and a ferret. Most of the cats were difficult to find and

In New Orleans, Lt. Randy Covey rescues a pet from this second floor apartment destroyed by Hurricane Katrina.

would hide when we approached, so we would take the time to search all the likely cubbyholes they might be hiding in. Sometimes our report would say there were two cats, and we would find three, so we made sure we found everyone before leaving and resecuring the house.

A poor timid pit bull mix inadvertently locked herself in a bathroom some time during the past week. She tried chewing a hole through the sheet rock, and she had bitten on the water connection to the toilet, causing water to spray continuously in a sprinkler pattern. She was afraid of us at first, but once she was out of the house she was a happy girl, jumping up on us and wriggling her body with joy.

We saw an emotional reuniting of the owner of the feed store with his 3 dogs and iguana. His house was in the flood zone and he thought they had all drowned. When he saw his dogs, he broke down crying.

DAY 6

We have been receiving e-mails and messages from the wonderful people in Portland, offering words of encouragement and thanking us for our efforts here in New Orleans…it really is a team effort and knowing that so many people are supporting us and counting on us to do our part is helping us maintain our momentum. Thanks!

DAY 7

The news from the base shelter was that 2,000 animals, critical mass at the shelter, had been reached. An independent rescue group had brought in 200 dogs unexpectedly. Just imagine the impact on any shelter of 200 dogs!

DAY 8

We heard dogs barking from a house not on our call list. When Casey and Randy finally located them (after jumping a few fences) they were so happy for human contact that they didn't pay much attention to the food and water we gave them, even though their bowls were empty! Our orders for the day were to feed and water in place; … leaving them behind was tearing us all up.

DAY 9

OHS has earned a reputation as an organization that will remain flexible and comply with any request that contributes to the success of the entire operation. I'm so proud of our team!

In our most dramatic rescue of the day, we were just leaving a factory where recovery workers gave us a rabbit they had found and put in a box. As we were getting back into our truck, we heard a bark from a house across the street. We approached. All we could see was a nose, no two noses, no, three big noses lifting the blinds in an effort to look out of the window at us! After quickly gaining access through the door, the three Rottweilers greeted us with wagging bodies and slobbery kisses!

As we were preparing to leave, Casey reminded us that we needed to clear the rest of the house…and proved again his value as a member of our rescue team. In the back corner, lying in the filth and clutter of two weeks' worth of Rottweiler survival camp, was an older male barely hanging on to life.

He bobbed his head with as much energy as he could muster as we rolled him onto a blanket and lifted him into our field stretcher (bottom half of a large dog crate) and put him in the air-conditioned cab of our truck.

As it was near the end of our day, we were likely this dog's last chance at survival...we took him immediately to the veterinarian at the triage center and helped as she gave him fluids in both the front and back leg and stabilized him. The feeling of watching that dog make a dramatic turnaround from lethargy to awareness is beyond description!

DAY 10

Our goal had changed to trying to maintain the animals in their homes, if possible, by providing food and water.... In order to save time and reach as many pets as possible, we did not perform exhaustive searches to locate all the whiskers and noses, but did the best we could and left the house secured with up to 2 weeks' supply of food and water.

DAY 11

As I walk through the parking lot to get from Barn 5 to the dog walking area, I am constantly impressed to see how many animal groups and people from all over the US are here to help the animals.... It does my heart good to see how much people care about these animals' welfare—and not just these people but all the people who have donated money and food and supplies to take care of these wonderful animals caught up in such a terrible disaster.

It is an awesome honor and responsibility to be here caring for these pets. It is also a very emotional experience. I helped the check-in process of a few that stand out in my mind. One was an emaciated female beagle who was very sweet. She had an ID on her

collar, so hopefully her owners will be able to be found soon. She was so weak I had to carry her through each stage of the check-in process, and as I gently carried her, she would rest her tired head on my shoulder. I rested my cheek on her forehead, and I think it brought both of us comfort.

"We needed the very best to do these rescues. The animals are scared and stressed and hungry."—Melissa Rubin, HSUS animal rescue coordinator, on OHS Technical Animal Rescue Team

Returning to Portland from New Orleans, team leader Randy Covey briefs reporters on the effects of Hurricane Katrina on domestic animals.

INCLUDING YOUR PETS IN DISASTER PREPAREDNESS PLANS

OHS encourages pet owners to plan ahead and stock an emergency kit to help keep pets safe in a disaster or emergency situation:

Assemble a pet survival kit and be prepared to evacuate

In order to contain and control your pets during an evacuation, you'll need a sturdy harness and leash for each dog and a carrier for each cat. The cat carrier should be large enough to serve as a temporary apartment for your cat. Pre-pack your pet's kit in a backpack for ease in transportation and include supplies for at least one week. Include current photos of your pets in case they get lost. Include dry food, a manual can opener for any canned food, clumping cat litter, drinkable water, serving dishes, small litter box, litter scoop, and plastic bags for waste disposal. A pet first aid kit is essential. Include any medications and medical records (stored in a waterproof container). Include information on feeding schedules, medical conditions, behavior problems, and the name and number of your veterinarian in case you have to foster or board your pets. You can also include pet beds or favorite toys, if easily transportable.

Tag, microchip, and photograph your pets

Current pet identification is the single most important thing you can do to help ensure that you will be reunited with a lost pet. Make certain your pet (even an indoors-only cat) is wearing a collar with visible identification tags with your phone number. A microchip implant is a secure form of identification that can't be lost. Be sure to carry a photograph with you to increase the likelihood of finding a missing pet. TIP: Take and store photos of your pets on your mobile phone.

Get to know your neighbors

Your neighbors may be home when a disaster hits and may be your best resource for evacuating your pets if you are unable to reach your home.

Have an alternative-shelter plan for your pets

If you must evacuate your home, do not leave your pets behind. If it is unsafe for you to remain, then it is unsafe for your pets as well. In a widespread emergency, the Red Cross sets up shelters to deal with human needs, but only service dogs are permitted inside. Therefore, you will need to have a separate shelter plan for your pets. Friends and family residing outside your immediate area are a possibility. Check with them to see if they would be willing to help shelter your pets. Contact hotels and motels outside your local area to check their policies on accepting pets and restrictions on number, size and species. Ask if "no pet" policies can be waived in an emergency. Keep a list of "pet friendly" places, including phone numbers, with your disaster supplies. Make a list of boarding facilities and veterinarians who could shelter animals in an emergency; include 24-hour phone numbers.

Be prepared to shelter pets in need

Giving temporary shelter to misplaced pets during a disaster saves lives. If you do take in a lost dog or cat, make sure to let rescue organizations know so that the animal can be reunited with its family.

Help emergency workers help your pets

Use a rescue sticker alert to let emergency responders know that pets are inside your home. Make sure the sticker is visible to rescue workers, and that it includes the types and number of pets in your household and your veterinarian's phone number. If you evacuate with your pets, (if time allows) write "EVACUATED" across the stickers so rescue workers don't delay by looking for pets who have already been evacuated.

Today, OHS has 60 FEMA-certified staff and volunteers who remain available to respond in case of emergency such as floods in Missouri, devastating wildfires in California, mudslides in Washington State, or the potentially devastating earthquake we call "The Big One" right here at home.

Wildlife

Domesticated animals and livestock are not the only concerns at OHS. At OHS in 1992, Sharon Harmon, co-author of a book titled *Living with Wildlife*, offered nonlethal solutions to problems involving wildlife. That July, she and Executive Director Dale Dunning also told the board about cruelties involved in raising elk so their antlers could be harvested, as well as abusive methods used in raising and showing Tennessee Walking horses. Dunning and Harmon assisted that same month in putting together an Exotics Symposium in Salem. Dunning also used the July board meeting to educate board members about elk ranching. Dunning told the board that OHS was in a position to spearhead an effort to stop elk ranching in Oregon. Pending investigation cases in August 1992 included pet store trading in wildlife.

Then operations director, Sharon Harmon made sure this elephant named Tiki received excellent care before appearing in the Portland Opera's 1989 production of *Aida*.

Pet Overpopulation/Spay & Neuter

Too many pets; not enough people to adopt them. For so many years, animal welfare organizations have wrangled with this problem. Practical issues, such as what to do with the excess of animals needing homes, jousted with emotional issues—such as what to do with all those animals. It took OHS many years to achieve this outcome, but today OHS saves 98 percent of all animals entering the shelter. The Portland Metro area receives national recognition for its exceptional save rate. In 2016, 95 percent of all pets entering our community's major shelters, public and private, found homes.

OHS joined forces with local veterinarians to combat pet overpopulation.

But the road to this impressive statistic was long and bumpy. All kinds of options were considered. In 1941, the OHS board voted to forbid cat castration. Allowing dogs in heat to run freely was against the law in 1948, but enforcement was lax. The OHS board agreed to urge police to arrest offenders. In 1964, the board proposed constructing a "dog port" so that dogs could be held there on heavy pickup days, instead of being immediately euthanized, as had been the practice in the past. That same December, 365 dogs were euthanized as they were brought in. In January of 1965, seven or eight dogs were crowded into each kennel, 148 dogs in all. At a meeting of the American Humane Association, representatives of the San Francisco SPCA had described their practice of keeping dogs considered fit for adoption for three days. If not taken into new homes by then, new dogs would be moved into the kennels in their place. OHS took some time in early 1965 to think about this course of action. There was also discussion of the advice from Charles Friedrichs of the AHA that no female cat or dog be allowed to leave a shelter until it had been spayed. He also recommended altering male dogs and cats.

In 1966, Mrs. Thelma Basowski, representing Friends of Animals, a national organization of humanitarians dedicated to reducing the surplus of unwanted dogs and cats by spaying females and altering males, asked to go before the board and explain how OHS could assist. Friends of Animals held that it was more humane to euthanize female dogs and cats than allow them to be adopted by people who had no intention of spaying the animals. The OHS board thought it would not be practical for the Society to join in the program at the time, but OHS did agree to distribute brochures from Friends of Animals, explaining that that group would pay part of the cost to spay or neuter a pet, with each dog leaving OHS. In September, the board also voted to contribute $20 a month to pay for Friends of Animals' advertisements in *The Oregonian*.

By December, 1967, there was growing recognition among the board that a spay and neuter program could help curtail the suffering that went along with a surplus of unwanted, sometimes starving animals. But other board members insisted that OHS was doing its part by helping Friends of Animals.

In 1972, more than 80,000 animals passed through the OHS shelter.

In 1973, the ASPCA became the first major shelter system to require that adopters agree to have their new pet spayed or neutered. OHS continued to remind low-income families that they could apply for reduced spaying fees through Friends of Animals.

So the abundance of unadopted pets continued. At a Saturday Market in 1983, OHS volunteer Andrea Wall spotted two homeless people playing with a puppy. Later, she found the puppy dead in a dumpster. To make matters worse, she saw people giving away litters of puppies as if they were free samples of laundry detergent.

The results of a 1998 study by the National Animal Control Association were not surprising to OHS. The year-long study of surrendered animals found that:

- **Two out of three unwanted dogs came from a friend or neighbor and had been obtained free.**
- **Most had been acquired under 12 weeks of age and had been kept less than six months.**

- **More than 54 percent were given up because of a change in the owner's lifestyle or because the owner thought he had an animal problem.**
- **A large percentage are given up for economic reasons— the owner "just couldn't afford the pet anymore."**

Things were starting to change. That same year, OHS announced the beginning of an interest-free Spay and Neuter Loan program to give financial assistance to pet owners for the sterilization of family pets. The loan fund, created in response to the pressures of the economic recession, would be administered by OHS and Animal Aid, Inc. Eligibility was income-based, and loans had to be repaid within six months.

At OHS, officials had heard every excuse in the world for not spaying or neutering an animal. A 1985 public service announcement from OHS took aim at these rationalizations: "I've been meaning to get her spayed, I just haven't gotten around to it!" "One litter won't hurt!" "I thought it cost too much!"

In 1990 alone, more than 11,000 dogs and cats were "humanely destroyed" at OHS because they were unwanted. The following year, after trustee Elaine Tanzer attended a pet overpopulation conference, the board passed a motion to endorse and initiate the adoption of formal governmental limitations on the breeding of cats and dogs in Portland and Multnomah County. Following through on this idea, a bill was introduced in the legislature in 1991 that would mandate sterilization of all dogs and cats adopted from any humane society, animal shelter or pound statewide.

> We endure because we are willing to fight for the defenseless creatures that we serve, and we know what we want for the future. We want to be working in an environment where we no longer take the lives of defenseless creatures because a disposable society doesn't want them.
>
> ~ OHS Director Dale Dunning, 1991

More progress came in 1992, with the launch of a major spay/neuter public relations campaign. Forty-four billboards popped up around Portland. Public Service Announcements played on local TV. Area veterinarians also joined in. The OHS Pet Overpopulation Committee met with representatives of Scamps pet stores, who had expressed interest in helping to place OHS pets. Scamps personnel said they were willing to abide by OHS spay and neuter requirements. The Pet Overpopulation Committee also arranged to work with Petco stores to facilitate adoptions by OHS volunteers.

But pet overpopulation problem persisted. In July, 1992, OHS received 1231 cats, 1072 of which were deemed suitable for adoption. That month, 913 cats were euthanized and 157 were adopted. In the same month, OHS received 571 dogs, of which 271 were eligible for adoption. July, 1992, saw 376 dogs euthanized at OHS, and 140 adopted. The next month, a candlelight vigil was held at Waterfront Park to observe the vast number of animals killed each year due to overpopulation.

With the catchy acronym of SNAP, the Spay/Neuter Assistance Program began in March 1993. This new OHS effort aimed to reduce cat overpopulation through financial assistance to people unable to afford the surgery, including people on low or fixed incomes, seniors, and people who rely on public assistance. The Portland Veterinary Medical Association unanimously approved the spay/neuter assistance program and OHS provided $20,000 in funding. SNAP's almost overnight success rate of 99 percent meant that the program was reinstated in 1994 with an additional $10,000 along with a $5,000 challenge.

Meantime, the public service announcement push continued. A 1998 message from OHS proclaimed: "Spayed or neutered animals are better companions, lead healthier lives, and are far less likely to roam or bite. Spayed or neutered pets do not lead to homeless puppies and kittens." That year, 88 percent of dogs and 50 percent of cats at OHS were adopted; more than 11,000 animals were received. The society placed 3960 cats and kittens and 712 other animals. In all, the number of adoptions rose 25 percent over the previous year.

At last, as the new millennium dawned, OHS took the step of requiring all adopted pets to be spayed

> Please, make the necessary arrangements right now to have your cat or dog altered. We all must stop this vicious cycle from repeating itself. Don't let your animal litter!
>
> ~ OHS Summer 1986 Newsletter

and neutered. Some had been spayed or neutered before admission, while others awaiting adoption were done as a courtesy by local veterinarians.

To adopt a still-fertile animal, a prospective owner was required to sign a legally binding contract and leave a $30 to $40 deposit. In cases where there might be doubt as to whether a new owner would fulfill the contract, the pet was sent directly to a veterinarian to be sterilized before the new owner took possession. The results were better than good. Combined with an aggressive tracking and follow-up program, this process achieved a 98 percent compliance rate.

All of the major animal-related organizations in the Portland/Vancouver metro area came together in 2006 to form the Animal Shelter Alliance of Portland (ASAP), thanks to the leadership and collaboration of co-founders Joyce Briggs and Britta Bavaresco. ASAP, with offices at OHS, aims to address pet overpopulation, reduce shelter intake and end unnecessary euthanasia. Three years later, in 2009, OHS and its alliance partners won major funding from PetSmart Charities that enabled them to begin Spay & Save. This targeted spay/neuter program sterilizes 10,000 cats annually from low-income households, as well as feral cats. Each year, approximately 5,000 cats receive services at the OHS Holman Medical Center.

It may sound like sensational self-promotion, but in truth it is impossible to overstate the success of this collaborative work.

The 95 percent save rate for cats and dogs has made the Portland area one of the safest communities for pets in the nation.

Since 2010, ASAP member agencies have saved every healthy and treatable pet entering our community's shelters. This accomplishment was recognized with a $1 million Lifesaving Award from Maddie's Fund. Since the inception of ASAP, euthanasia in Portland's shelters has dropped by 90 percent. The 95 percent save rate for cats and dogs has made the Portland area one of the safest communities for pets in the nation.

Of all the thousands of cats served by Spay & Save, Soma was the first.

32

Euthanasia

No matter what euphemism is substituted—"putting to sleep," for instance, or "putting down"—this term shoots right up your spine, straight to your moral cortex. In fact the word itself, "euthanasia"— translates as "a good death." And sometimes, as painful as it may be to address or accept, that is the best option to hope for. Today, euthanasia is a last-choice decision. The OHS veterinary team will only "sign off" on an animal when a reasonable pet owner would make the same choice. In fact, euthanasia today is sufficiently rare at OHS that two areas of the shelter built just 20 years earlier for euthanasia services have now been repurposed for specialized medical services designed to save lives, not end them.

Looking back, attitudes and practices were markedly different. A 1924 classified ad promised that animals would be "painlessly electrocuted" at OHS. In 1940, the board expressed appreciation to one Mr. Palmer for the gift of a collar he had fashioned out of copper, promising that death would be easier in the electric chamber. In 1948, the stated policy was that "dogs shall be disposed of as quickly as it is consistent to do so."

By 1964, the superintendent was protesting to the board because he had to euthanize 70 dogs in one day, simply because he had no place to put them. Frances Blakely countered with these reassuring words: "I am sure Mr. Zimmer has never allowed a so-called good dog, or one that had a chance of getting a home, to be put to sleep. The surplus of dogs that does rise in astounding numbers which are put away are usually little sore-eyed female puppies; old dogs with skin disease or just the common overabundance of mongrel females that have little or no chance of being sold or given away."

A new process called "Euthanair" came into use in 1968. Animals were taken daily in a trailer to the city incinerator for disposal. When asked by the public how animals were euthanized, OHS employees were instructed to explain that "the animals are taken up to the equivalent of 55,000 feet in altitude in a very short time." This procedure, employees were told to explain, quickly renders an animal unconscious, much like a high-flying pilot without an oxygen mask. They were admonished to add that Euthanair "has been proven by veterinarians throughout the United States as the most humane method of euthanasia."

A 1979 article in *Your Animal's Friend* argued this chamber method was preferable to death by lethal injection, as it was less stressful for humane technicians. The article averred, "Your SPCA is keeping an open mind on alternative euthanasia methods. There is substantial evidence that the Euthanair chamber meets the humane requirements of being quick, painless and humane." But protesters picketing at OHS disagreed, and eventually their sentiments prevailed. In 1980, OHS implemented what it called "the most humane form of euthanasia—the injection method, using sodium pentobarbital." By 1989, OHS was requiring that all OHS kennel employees become certified euthanasia technicians within six months of coming to work at OHS.

Still, OHS has worked tirelessly to end needless euthanasia, mainly by bringing the supply of animals into balance with the number of available homes. The OHS "End Petlessness" campaign has made it a model for the rest of the country.

Trees, gardens and the sound of flowing water grace the entrance to the animal cemetery on the grounds of OHS.

33

Memorial Gardens

Following a model she had begun in her own backyard on Palatine Hill, Mrs. F. W. Swanton established the shelter's pet cemetery during her tenure as general manager in 1918. The legendary Bobbie of Silverton, subject of books, movies and extensive media acclaim, found his final resting spot in the OHS Memorial Garden. At his well-attended memorial service, Portland Mayor Robert Earl Riley remarked that "Bobbie, that collie whose love for his master drove him through storm and cold, hunger and hardship half way across the continent and he reached his home on foot months later. Bobbie symbolizes all that is loyal and noble in the dog world."

Bobbie's house in 1987.

Bobbie of Silverton

Also spending eternity in the Memorial Garden is Peggy Borneo, the pet orangutan of Mrs. E. Hauber, a Portland woman who had big dreams for her hairy primate companion. Only a few days before Peggy died in 1929, her owner had signed a contract to have Peggy appear in movies that would have made Peggy a very rich orangutan. Peggy was dressed in rompers like a child, had her own chair and slept in a bed with sheets, pillowcases and coverlet. Peggy tooled around in a kiddy car and frolicked in a backyard sandbox. Her funeral was a grand and elaborate affair, and Peggy was laid to rest in a lavish white, satin-lined casket.

The cemetery at OHS is the oldest pet burial grounds west of the Mississippi.

After their beloved pet Smokey Hungate died at age 12 in 1955, his owners, Helen and Clyde Fenton, sent donations for nearly 50 years so that flowers could be placed on Smokey's grave. This practice continued into the 21st century, even after the Fentons had moved to another state. Retiring Board President Homer Angell waxed eloquent about the Pet Memorial Garden in 1963: "Benches, flanked by tall evergreens and a rose garden, invite guests with a love of animals to spend some peaceful moments in contemplation of God's handiwork here in the garden of pleasant memories, above a tiny lake in view of snowcapped mountains across the mighty Columbia River."

Another animal celebrity in the OHS pet cemetery is Dolly, a war mascot brought back from Flanders fields by J. A. Kraft of Portland. A poor little dog named Jiggs died of a broken heart when his owner went to jail sometime in the 1930s. Queenie was a stately shepherd whose toenails had been pulled out, according to OHS records, "by some fiend in Willamina, Ore." Mrs. Swanton's own two cats are buried there as well, along with canaries, goldfish and the occasional reptile. The garden got so crowded that in 1940, its size was doubled, and plans were made to install the fountain at the entrance, where it sits today.

Future Gov. Tom McCall speaking at the dedica of the OHS animal mausoleum and columbar

A stone in the memorial gardens pays honor to all pets OHS has served.

"Benches, flanked by tall evergreens and a rose garden, invite guests with a love of animals to spend some peaceful moments..."

~ Howard Angell, 1963

Once again, OHS was setting a national example. The mausoleum and columbarium for burial of animal ashes was the first such combination for pets in the United States. A third mausoleum was added in 1966, donated by an anonymous woman who stipulated that it be built on the same specifications that the Health Department requires for human remains. Even though the columbarium contained 2,000 niches for ashes, and the 144-unit mausoleum had been built for 66 embalmed pets, by the early 1970s, the garden was getting crowded. Already, the cemetery with 2,250 pet graves was fully occupied.

So in 1973, the Society dedicated two more large mausoleums on the second Sunday in June, also known as Pet Memorial Day. By that winter, an additional 1,500 plots had been opened for pet burials.

Renovations began again in 1982, including replacement of above-ground plaques with ground level markers to make the cemetery easier to care for. Yet another expansion was underway, too. A human memorial was dedicated in 1992, honoring a young woman named Aimee Wood who lost her life a year earlier while attempting to rescue an injured dog from the freeway. Roses continue to bloom in abundance in gardens long maintained by OHS employee Terri Roush. Even after her retirement, Roush visits frequently to tend the beloved roses that have twice won the Mayor's Trophy during Rose Festival.

WEDDING GONE TO THE DOGS

The Rose Garden is more than a place to say farewell to loved companions. The headline on a June 1993 wedding story read "Tying the Leash, Er...the Knot." When newly retired OHS adoption counselor Ruthye Dennis was married in the society's Rose Garden, staff dogs served as attendants, and wedding bells hung suspended from leashes. A pair of Rottweilers named Kaiser and Berlin pulled the newlyweds in a ribbon and balloon-bedecked cart as they made their way from the garden to the reception in the auditorium. About 100 guests attended this first-ever wedding at the Oregon Humane Society. The story of this unusual wedding venue ran in newspaper across the country and was featured on CNN.

Animal Crime Forensics Center

A professional forensics center will allow OHS to conduct meticulous investigations, gather unimpeachable evidence, and bring unassailable expertise to court to provide justice for animals in cruelty cases.

Baxter
Cruelty Case Survivor

Community Teaching Hospital

Our goal is to provide affordable veterinary care to the public, especially those with limited financial means, to preserve families and prevent homelessness.

Snowball
Beloved Family Member

Behavior & Training Center

The new center will build on the success of our current behavior and training program, and provide a low-stress, healing environment to help animals love and trust again.
For some animals, this will be a life-saving intervention.

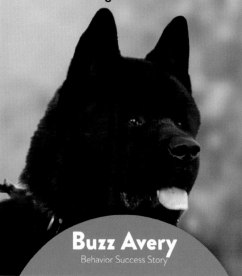

Buzz Avery
Behavior Success Story

Dedicated Rescue Center

A dedicated animal rescue center means being able to say "yes" to cases of animal cruelty and neglect, with the flex space, resources, and expertise to respond at a moment's notice.

Sunshine
Rescued From Neglect

Animals cannot tell us what they need. Sure, they have ways of communicating with us. But for the really important things, they need someone to speak for them. For a hundred and fifty years, the Oregon Humane Society has been that voice.

If animals are being abused, we stand up for them. If they need homes, we find one. If they need a little extra time and patience, we give it to them. We never give up on animals and because of that, Portland is now one of the safest places for pets to thrive.

We're incredibly proud of our success, and it would be tempting to sit back and rest on our laurels, but that is not who we are. As CEO Sharon Harmon puts it, "It's our obligation to do more." It's time for OHS to build on our success and do even more for the animals who need us. Looking to the future, we see three areas where we can make a huge impact:

- **Keeping pets and families together**

- **Preventing animal cruelty**

- **Caring for rescued animals.**

We are proposing four new initiatives as a response to the challenges these areas present. They are based on real problems that we are seeing right now and are designed to make a big difference right away. These bold programs comprise a $30-million initiative that will further our mission to be a voice for the animals. We call it the New Road Ahead, and it will take all of us working together to move our vision forward.

Our Vision

The field of animal welfare is changing rapidly in many parts of the country. For shelters on the leading edge of this change, it is an exciting and challenging time as we are finally approaching the end of pet overpopulation. Now that the predominant issue of pet overpopulation is controlled, we can turn our attention to other more intractable issues impacting animal welfare. OHS intends to confront suffering in all its insidious forms, from the heartbreak of surrendering a pet to untreated medical conditions, and of course the most egregious of all—intentional cruelty and neglect.

The New Road Ahead offers four cornerstone solutions to these challenges: 1) Community Teaching Hospital, 2) Dedicated Animal Rescue Center, 3) Animal Crime Forensics Center, and 4) Behavior and Training Center.

Community Teaching Hospital

Having a pet is a serious responsibility, not just emotionally but financially as well. Even basic veterinary care such as checkups and vaccinations can be expensive, but when a beloved cat or dog becomes sick or injured, the medical costs can be out of reach for otherwise good homes.

More and more animals are surrendered to OHS because the owners can't afford veterinary treatment for illnesses and injuries, and that's heartbreaking. No caring person should ever have to give up what may be their only family member because the costs are too high.

OHS already has a state-of-the-art medical center in partnership with Oregon State University College of Veterinary Medicine.

We are in conversations with OSU to expand this program so that we may offer this rotation to OSU veterinary students at all year-levels.

Right now it's a teaching hospital that cares for OHS-owned animals, but it could be so much more. We want to expand the current Holman Medical Center to offer veterinary care to the public—and especially to those with limited financial means.

We believe we can preserve families and restore health by offering affordable medical services as a humane solution to pet homelessness. Our goal is to provide veterinary care to all who need it, utilizing a sustainable business model to preserve the animal-human bond while reducing the suffering of untreated medical conditions.

A Dedicated Animal Rescue Center

Fighting against animal cruelty is what OHS is founded on. While we're always going to help individual animals, the reality of our world today means that we also need to be ready to help large numbers of animals all at once. OHS is the only Oregon agency that can effectively manage cases involving several hundred animals. We are frequently asked by agencies across the state to assist with cruelty cases involving large numbers of pets, in addition to cases investigated by our own team of commissioned police officers, forensic veterinarians, and credentialed police support staff. Large-scale animal rescues can occur at any time, with little to no prior notice. If a hundred dogs are living in deplorable conditions, they need our help now—not in a couple of weeks when we've found space for them. Bringing them to the main shelter means displacing animals who are waiting to be adopted. And in many cases, rescued animals are considered

evidence in a criminal proceeding and can't be adopted until the criminal case is resolved. That can mean a stay of a year or more.

A dedicated rescue center will allow us to say "yes" when the need arises. Immediately and without delay whenever a large group of animals need our help, we can have the space, resources, and expertise ready to respond on a moment's notice. The sooner we get the animals out of danger, the sooner we can help them heal and bring their abusers to justice.

Animal Crime Forensics Center

As the only law enforcement agency in Oregon focused solely on animal cruelty, OHS is frequently asked to assist other agencies in the forensic examination of living and deceased pets to detect and prove criminal cases. These agency requests for assistance along with our own cases result in thousands of examinations each year.

Securing a conviction against abusers is no longer guaranteed—not when there are attorneys who specialize in defending those accused of animal cruelty and are committed to getting the charges dropped, so we have to be ready for them.

A professional forensics center will allow OHS staff to conduct meticulous investigations, gather unimpeachable evidence, and bring unassailable expertise to court. This will enable OHS to move cases through the judicial system more quickly, resulting in animals being held for less time as evidence. A recent case involving 121 dogs took 23 months to conclude, with convictions on all counts. Two years is far too long for dogs to have their lives on hold, spent in a shelter waiting for justice.

Behavior and Training Center

OHS aims to find a warm, loving home for every animal that comes through the doors. For fluffy kittens and adorable puppies, that's easy. But for animals rescued from abusive situations, more is required.

These pets require socialization and training to be available for adoption by our clients. Our certified trainers work with these pets to help them recover from abuse and trauma, or just simply a lack of love. Many rescued animals are extremely fearful. Many have never been loved. Before they can go to a good home, they have to learn how to live in the world. Sometimes that means learning to trust people for the first time in their lives, and that doesn't happen overnight.

This program will build on the success of our current behavior and training program. It will provide a low-stress, healing environment for rescued animals, as well as for shelter animals who are older and have medical or behavioral issues that are making it harder for us to place them in homes. For many animals, this will be a lifesaving intervention.

Currently this program is housed in multiple areas of our shelter that were not designed for employee safety, long term stays or rehabilitation. Our experience has shown that given a quiet, low-traffic area designated for high risk dogs we can save them. If we rescue them from cruel treatment we owe it to them to give them every chance to trust people again and find a kind home.

Conclusion

One hundred and fifty years ago compassionate Portland citizens banded together to stop neglect and abuse of horses, dogs, cats and children. They recognized the right of all sentient beings to pursue a healthy existence. Thus began the Oregon Humane Society.

Today OHS stands as a champion of animal welfare throughout our state and beyond. We protect animals with cruelty investigations. We rescue animals from danger. We provide animal (and human) behavioral training. We provide state-of-the art veterinary care to shelter pets in partnership with OSU. We work with legislators to ensure humane treatment for all animals. And of course, we work tirelessly to find caring human companions through our adoption services.

The future is about ensuring compassion and preventing suffering for all animals. We will rise to meet today's challenges, and we invite you to join us.

By Stacy Bolt, on assignment for OHS

Appendices

APPENDIX A

OREGON HUMANE SOCIETY BOARD PRESIDENTS

1872-74	Bernard Goldsmith
1875-79	Unknown
1880	Rev. A. L. Lindsley
1880-82	Mayor David P. Thompson
1883-98	Rev. Thomas Lamb Eliot
1899-1901	David P. Thompson
1902	Charles H. Woodward
1903-7	Judge Alfred F. Sears, Jr.
1907	Frederick K. Townsend
1908	H. M. Cake
1909-11	August Berg
1911-13	Robert F. Tucker
1914-19	Albert Cowperthwait
1919-20	Judge Otto J. Kraemer
1921-26	Col. Ernest Hofer
1927-30	Pierre M. Baldwin
1931-2	Mrs. Lillie D. Thomas
1933	S. H. Palmer
1934-47	Harry Daniel
1948-55	Harvey Wells
1956-60	Thomas B. Winship
1961-63	Homer D. Angell
1964-67	Lawrence C. Shaw
1968-72	R. Robert Smith
1973-76	William H. Boland
1977	Mrs. James W. (Joan)Morrell
1978-79	William H. Boland
1980-81	Peter Koerner
1982-83	William T. Rutherford
1984-87	Tim Jones
1988-89	Dolorosa Margulis
1990-91	Ernest C. Swigert
1992-93	William Parkhurst
1993-95	John Deering
1996-97	David Gearing
1998	Laird Goodman, D.V.M.
1999-2000	Stuart Soren
2001	Herb Goodman
2002-03	Michael J. Bragg
2004	Harvey N. Black
2005-06	Marveita Redding
2007-09	Betty Norrie
2010-12	Dave Hansen
2013	Reginald R. Eklund
2014-2017	Marc F. Grignon
2017-	John Gomez

APPENDIX B

TOP VOLUNTEERS

Feel the Love/End Petlessness Award

2007	Kat Hamlin
2008	Colleen Foley
2009	Ken Wells
2010	Simone Steib
2011	Joanne Hodgdon
2012	Sandy Heusch
2013	Susan Davis
2014	Jill Hurtley
2015	Margaret Spear
2016	Karl Keener
2017	Carol Christiansen

Volunteer's Choice Award

2003	Marty Brzana
2004	James McDougald
2005	Ken Wells
2006	Jeanne Bracken
2007	Carrie Brownstein
2008	Roger Price
2009	Miriam Moore
2010	Dorma Mammano
2011	Lois Johnson
2012	Sarah Maher
2013	Alicia Dickerson
2014	Sherry Adams
2015	Joanne Hodgdon
2016	Ed McClaran
2017	Denise Kinstetter

Volunteer of the Year Award

2003	Mary Millard
2004	Ken Wells
2005	Stephanie Vaughn
2006	Rhonda Brande
2007	Jennifer Shirley
2008	Janet Bates
2009	Anika Moje
2010	Marty Ramirez
2011	Kathy Lillis
2012	Eldon Loewe
2013	Sandy Kraft
2014	Candace and Bill Bailey
2015	Tim Hurtley
2016	Bobbi Waggoner
2017	René Pizzo

Volunteer Lifetime Achievement Award

2003	Karin Cereghino
2004	Barbra Bader
2005	Roberta Cobb
2006	Ernie and Sherri Brown
2007	Mary Huey
2008	Charles Aubin
2009	Dianne Pengue
2010	Lou Chapman
2011	Diane Hogan
2012	Laura Klink
2013	Julie Honse
2014	Carolyn Gressel
2015	Joe Cereghino
2016	Marty Brzana
2017	Teresa Leap

TABLE OF FIGURES

OHS acknowledges with thanks the following institutions and individuals who have generously shared images reproduced in Pioneering Compassion. The remaining illustrations have come from the archives of the Oregon Humane Society.

LeslieAnn Butler: p. 40.

GoogleEarth: p. 52.

Jeffrey Hastings: dust jacket (portrait of Mary Henry).

Kristine Hoebermann: dust jacket (portrait of Elizabeth Mehren).

Tim Hurtley: pp. 65, 84 and 122.

Oregon Historical Society: pp. 17 (at right), 18, 19, 20, 21, 22, 34, 47, 70 (at left), 92, 129, 130 (at right), 141, and 142.

The Oregonian/Oregon Journal: pp. 23, 27, 59, 63, 68, 69, 121, 125 (Chuck Von Wald, photographer), and 143 (Herb Alden, photographer).

City of Portland Archives: pp. 26, 48, 52 (1925 aerial), 115, and 124.

Reed College: pp. 13 and 103.

Special thanks also to the University of Oregon Aerial Photography Research Service for assistance with historic aerial imagery.

ENDNOTES

Research for this volume was conducted through personal interviews and by reviewing materials in the Oregon Humane Society's archives. Additional information was found at the Oregon Historical Society Research Library, which houses a significant collection of Oregon Humane Society records; the Multnomah County Library; the City of Portland Archives; Historic Oregonian newspapers; and The Special Collections & Archives of the Reed College Library.

p. 14   Joyce Briggs, personal communication, using American Veterinary Medical Association calculation tools found at *https://www.avma.org/KB/Resources/Statistics/Pages/Market-research-statistics-US-pet-ownership.aspx*.

p. 21   "Exploring close prehistoric relationship between human and dog," *http://www.research.ualberta.ca/en/dogs*

p. 27   William Shanahan, "Law of Kindness." *The Oregonian*, Feb. 7, 1888, p. 3.

p. 28   Joseph Gaston, Portland, Oregon, *Its History and Builders* (S.J. Clarke, 1911).

p. 29   *Your Animal's Friend*, Fall/Winter 1980, p. 5.

p. 29   *OHS Magazine*, Fall/Winter 1993, p. 3.

p. 29   City of Portland, Oregon, Ordinance No. 19737.

p. 30   "Humane Sunday to Be Observed Today," *The Oregonian*, May 21, 1916, p. 13.

p. 32   *Your Animal's Friend*, I, 7, 1, Spring 1971.

p. 32   *Your Animal's Friend*, I, 3, 1, Spring 1973, p. 4.

p. 50   *Your Animals' Friend*, Sept. 1970, I, 5, 2, quoting report by Dr. H. Propp and Dr. C.S. Eakin, Assistant State Veterinarian.

p. 53   "67 Dogs Smother in Fire at Pound" *The Oregonian*, March 16, 1939, p. 59.

p. 54   OHS Board Minutes, Mar. 12, 1940.

p. 54   *Your Animal's Friend*, Winter 1977, p. 1.

p. 55   Merritt Clifton, Animals 24-7 "*http://www.animals24-7.org/2015/12/22/the-oregon-humane-society-what-a-world-class-shelter-looks-like/*

p. 61   *Your Animal's Friend*, Summer 1973, p. 8.

p. 63   "Fountains for Thirsty," Letter to the Editor, Shanahan, William,

p. 63   *The Oregonian*, July 4, 1906.

p. 69   OHS Education Dept. brochure—1990s.

p. 75   *OHS Magazine*, Fall 1999.

p. 84   OHS Executive Committee Minutes, Jan. 12, 1993.

p. 90   *OHS Speaks*, Fall 1985.

p. 98   *The Oregon Humane Society Speaks*, Summer 1985.

p. 99   *OHS Magazine*, Fall 1991.

p. 103   OHS Board Minutes, Sep. 17,1968.

p. 103   Zawistowski, Stephen, personal communication via electronic mail, May 28, 2016.

p. 105   Friends Forever ad, *OHS Magazine*, Spring 2000, p. 17.

p. 107   Dale Dunning, OHS President's board notes, June 16, 1992.

p. 115   1855 Dog license order from City of Portland; City of Portland Archives.

p. 117   Sharon Harmon, "Direct Line," *OHS Magazine*, Fall 1999, p. 3.

p. 123   Quoted in Emily Steward Leavitt, Animals and their legal rights, Animal Welfare Institute, 1968, 3rd edition 1978, p. 11.

p. 126   Sharon Harmon, "Legislative Action—A Tradition," *OHS Annual Report* 1993-4, p 22.

p. 146   OHS Board minutes, Feb. 18, 1964.

p. 153   OHS Executive Committee minutes, Dec. 10, 1991.

p. 159   "Animals Rest in Honored Graves," *The Oregonian*, March 22,1931, p. 58.

p. 129   "Investigations—A Long Tradition," *OHS Magazine*, Fall/Winter 1993-4, p. 17.

p. 132   OHS Board Minutes, Feb. 15, 1966.

p. 133   OHS Board Minutes, Mar. 10, 1964.

p. 133   OHS Board Minutes, Apr. 7, 1948.

p. 138   Hoarding of Animals Research Consortium, quoted by Animal Legal Defense Fund— *http://aldf.org/resources/laws-cases/animal-hoarding-case-study-vikki-kittles/*

p. 138   Harmon, "Legislative Action," OHS Annual Report 1993-4, p. 22.

p. 146   *Your Animal's Friend*, I, 7,1 (1971), p. 1.

p. 146   OHS Board packet, President's notes, Sept. 15, 1992.

p. 152   OHS Executive Committee minutes August 11, 1992.

p. 153   OHS Board minutes, May 17, 1966 and April 19, 1966.

p. 154   Lane & Zawistowski 2008, referenced in "The Development of Animal Shelters."

p. 155   *The Oregon Humane Society Speaks*, Summer 1985, p. 2.

p. 155   *The Oregon Humane Society Speaks*, Summer 1986.

p. 155   OHS Board minutes, February 18, 1992.

p. 157   *Your Animal's Friend*, Winter 1979.

p. 159   Robert Earl Riley, Speeches: the Oregon humane society; record date circa 12/31/1934; Box and folder numbers 23/51, Accession Number A2010-019.

p. 159   *OHS Magazine* Winter/Fall 1991, p. 2.